STREET WISE

STREET WISE

John Goodfellow

YWAM Publishing
A Ministry of Youth With A Mission
Seattle, Washington 98155

Streetwise

Published by YWAM Publishing, a division of Youth With A Mission; P. O. Box 55787, Seattle, WA 98155

All Scriptures are from the New International Version of the Bible unless stated in the text.

ISBN 0-92754-512-8

Printed in the United States of America

Dedication

To Floyd and Sally McClung,
For your love, friendship, and humble walk with God.

Acknowledgements

This book wouldn't have been written without the prayers, practical help, and support of some very dear people.

First, I want to thank my wife, Terry, for helping me find the time to work on the manuscript, and providing the fine detail my memory missed. I'm grateful, too, for Mandy Butcher's patience in freeing her husband, Andy, to spend so many evenings at the typewriter putting our conversations together. Andy took this on despite his already heavy workload as Editor of *Christian Family* magazine at that time.

I also want to thank Geoff Benge for all his work in preparing the manuscript for this American edition. Without him, this edition would not have been possible.

My sister, Trish, brother-in-law, Jamie, and Mom provided timely encouragement and comment as the project developed. Sister Joan helped in this way, too, as well as typing some of the manuscript along with Myrtle Thompson.

Finally, I am indebted to Floyd McClung for his initial spur to put pen to paper, in the hope and belief that telling this story may be a way that God will touch and change other people's lives in the way He has mine.

I have changed the actual names of a few of the people and places, where it seemed appropriate to do so. But most are identified, and all the incidents and experiences are recounted just as I remember they happened.

John Goodfellow

Table of Contents

1

Street Fighting Man

Working in a bar on Spain's tourist coast was everything I had been promised and hoped for: an endless round of alcohol and free sex that only made me thirst for more. If the pace got too hectic, there was always a plentiful supply of drugs to charge me up for another night of partying.

By day, the Crazy Horse Saloon was just another shabby building, hastily constructed from cheap, rough-sawn wood, with a large veranda facing the dusty street. It seemed out of place sitting two hundred yards from the beach at Santa Suzanna, a small seaside town just outside Lorette del Mar.

But as the sun went down, the Crazy Horse Saloon transformed into one of the top night spots for the young sun seekers who flooded into Spain on package vacations. Scores of young people from England, Holland, and Germany crowded nightly into the cavernous bar, where they noisily drank and danced until 2:00 a.m. or later.

For a small-time criminal with a drinking problem and a growing dislike for the hard work of bricklaying in the wet, cold British Midlands, it was a paradise. Two friends who were running the Crazy Horse Saloon for the summer season had asked me to join their bar staff, and I had been delighted to accept. Free drinks—for as long as we could stand on our feet—were an added bonus.

The tourist girls were impressed by our macho image. They had come from boring nine-to-five jobs in anonymous offices in gray cities, looking for a holiday romance. We were as close as they got.

At the end of each evening, a group of them waited behind, giggling and slightly the worse for wear. We paired off dispassionately before deciding which couples would use the staff quarters—a cramped, dirty bunk house at the rear of the bar—and which would go back to the girls' hotels, where we gave the night watchman a knowing leer as we crept past.

Most mornings I awoke wondering where I was, who I had been with, and where I could find a drink to ease the throbbing in my head. If I never exchanged names with the girl, it was fine with me; I didn't want to see her again, anyway. Once my passion was spent, I usually couldn't wait for her to get her clothes on and leave.

I usually stumbled out of bed around noon, then met up with my friends for a large breakfast, which we washed down with several beers. We swapped stories about the girls we had been with the night before, comparing notes like buyers at a cattle market. After this early afternoon breakfast, we napped for an hour or so on the beach, then went on our daily "propaganda patrol." We strutted along the beach, handing out leaflets that urged the sunbathers to come along to the Crazy Horse Saloon that evening.

We weren't working hard just for the fun of it. The fact was, the more customers there were, the more opportunity we had to rip them off or get them into bed—or both. It was as simple as that. We were eager for everyone who came to the saloon to spend as much as possible, so we whipped up the party atmosphere by joining in the dancing, kidding with the customers, and generally behaving as though we were having a great time. But as we did it, we always watched for the chance to coax an unwary girl away from her circle of friends, or to steal from someone.

One of the simplest ways to make money on the side was to shortchange the customers. As the evening wore on and the bar became packed to capacity with a sweaty throng, it was easy to delay returning a person's change. Finally, I got back to them and as I shortchanged them, made a vague excuse about being busy. Most often they didn't notice, and the secret pocket in my uniform was usually bulging with stolen notes by closing time.

I quietly hid away as much money as I could. I sometimes wondered if I could possibly stash any more money under the grubby mattress on my bunk, without someone getting too suspicious. I trusted that the other guys were like me, too tired, too stoned, or too drunk to notice my bulging mattress.

In an atmosphere charged with sex and alcohol, violence was never too far away. When it came, we welcomed it with open arms and clenched fists—it was the thing that made our job satisfaction complete. We recognized that if we won the reputation as the toughest team of bouncers on the coast, we would have less trouble in the bar, and would impress some of the girls with our toughness, not to mention the fact that we reveled in a good fight. As a result, we dealt with any problems ruthlessly and efficiently.

If someone began to create a scene in the bar,

perhaps over a girl, a spilled drink, or an unguarded remark, they were hustled outside and given a swift beating before being advised to leave. From our perspective, the cardinal sin in the bar was for a customer to hit a fellow waiter. From time to time, when one of us was a little slow in sorting out a situation, or was caught trying to get away with someone's change, it happened. Within seconds, the assailant was felled by two or three other waiter/bouncers.

Outside, the person was held down and viciously kicked and stomped. We broke arms, legs, and ribs, and laughed as our victims crawled away. As long as we didn't create a disturbance with the locals, the Spanish police didn't really care what happened at the bar.

Indeed, we weren't anxious to allow the locals into the saloon. It wasn't so much that we feared creating a situation with them, but since they weren't as free-spending as vacationers, they simply took up bar space and slowed down trade. We also had complaints that the Spanish men harassed girls in the bar, which brought us together in a muddled sort of patriotic gallantry. So we generally tried to discourage the Spaniards from staying too long in the bar—until one evening.

It was almost closing time, and the bar was virtually empty. As usual, the floor was awash in spilled beer, empty glasses, and cigarette butts. The air was thick with the smells of tobacco and cheap perfume. We were busy cleaning up so we could spend the rest of the night with the latest group of girls who milled around, waiting for us.

As we were about finished, a small group of Spanish men insisted they be served one last drink, and refused to take no for an answer. As we argued the point, one of the men grabbed an ashtray and brought it crashing down on a waiter's head.

The bar exploded in a flurry of kicks, punches, and curses. The men were outnumbered and soon fled, except for their leader. He was a bull of a man, and wild. It finally took four of us to subdue him. We battered him to the ground and dragged him outside, where we laid into him with our fists and boots. We left him groaning in the dust, and when he fell silent, I thought we'd killed him.

After we determined that he was still alive, we spit on him and headed back inside. The thrill of combat led to drinks all around, and inflated our view of ourselves as the meanest, toughest crew of bouncers around. We enjoyed our notoriety, and were greatly pleased at the way the customers held us in awe as the story of our fight was retold, being embellished each time.

A couple of weeks later, word filtered back that our victim had been badly hurt in the attack. He had been admitted to the hospital with severe internal injuries, a broken arm, fractured leg, and cracked ribs. He was a popular figure in the area, and the rumor was that a revenge attack was planned.

We took this threat seriously, and in our off-duty moments, fashioned ourselves a brutal arsenal to repel any would-be attacker. We had iron bars, bottles, bricks, and wooden clubs wrapped with barbed wire. I painstakingly carved jagged teeth into the end of a three-foot long wooden stake.

When we had finished putting together our arsenal, we posed for photographs, trying to out-boast each other as we demonstrated what we would do if called upon to use our weapons. We wore construction hard hats and big grins as we clutched our batons and bars, posing for the photographer.

For the next week, we were especially careful to

be on our guard, and meticulous about checking every visitor to the Crazy Horse Saloon. But as time passed, we lapsed into carelessness. Finally, one evening, another waiter grabbed my arm.

"Johnny, look over there in the corner," he shouted in my ear, raising his voice above the drumming disco beat.

"Where?" I turned and looked in the direction he was pointing. In a darkened corner of the bar, away from the dance floor, were two familiar faces. We scanned the room more closely, and to our horror, spotted two or three more young men who had been involved in the fight.

We held a hurried council of war at the bar, and decided to close early. The DJ offered some excuse, and we managed to usher everyone out. We locked and bolted the doors behind them, gathered together at the shuttered windows, then spotted a small group of men at the end of the street. Their wolf cries and shouts carried down the street as we reached behind the bar for our weapons.

All went quiet for a few minutes, and then our attackers assaulted the heavy door, using a log or bench as a battering ram. As soon as they burst through, we attacked, and a bloody brawl ensued in the darkened bar. Chairs were thrown and sticks swung. We managed to beat them back and then, suddenly, they bolted. Inflamed by the fighting, we whooped and hollered and ran out into the street after them.

As we turned the corner in pursuit, we realized what a dreadful mistake we had made. Another fifteen or more heavily-armed men stood before us. Now thirty angry young men confronted us. More stepped in behind us, blocking our escape. The twelve of us had run straight into a trap.

Fear and hatred swirled within me, fueling my arms. I swung my sharpened rod, lashing out in all directions. Everywhere around me in the gray moonlight, blurred bodies stumbled in a fog of violence. Screams of pain and shouts of fury mixed with the thud of wood and metal on flesh and bone.

We were totally outnumbered, angry people pushing in on all sides. A moment of rational thought burst through my mind: if I went down, I would never get up again—they wouldn't stop short of killing me! My blood ran cold.

A thick-set, curly-headed man lunged forward to smash an iron bar across my head. I jerked to one side and ducked his blow. I clenched my teeth and put every ounce of aggression I had into the savage swing of my heavy rod. It connected, shattering the man's cheekbone and jarring my hand painfully. I gave a satisfied yell before stepping forward and pulling back my rod for another strike. "Come on, who will be next?" I goaded.

The fear was gone. In its place was an ordered, calm appreciation of the pleasure of inflicting serious injury. I faced the next man who stepped into my path and, with grim enjoyment, assessed the best place to hit him to cause the maximum damage.

Suddenly it was quiet except for the gasping for breath, and raw terror was all around as we stood face to face. We were enemies, sharing a common thought—the fighting had transformed us into machines of violence.

The smell of violence intoxicated me and seemed to trigger my last safety valve. "Okay, let's go and get the dirty...!" I roared as I sprang forward, leading a charge at the surprised enemy.

Then pain burst across my face, and I felt something warm on my cheek—blood. A hurled brick had split my skin to the bone. Broken bottles, chains, iron bars, and all manner of other weapons were once again being wielded.

Triumph filled me as I saw our enemies start to break and run. It took me a few moments to realize that we weren't the reason for their flight. *La Garda* (the police) had arrived in force.

I dropped my stick and gently touched the wound on the side of my face. The fighting was over, but all I could think was how I wished I'd had the chance to hurt someone else before it had ended.

Not surprisingly, the Spanish authorities were not happy with us. But since the locals with whom we'd been fighting hadn't waited around to explain what had been going on, we fabricated a story about how we were defending ourselves from an attempted robbery.

I knew the police didn't believe us for a moment. But since there were no witnesses, they had no choice but to drop the matter.

For the next few weeks, we had a police escort wherever we went, to make sure there were no further "attempted robberies." As a result, our macho reputation was greatly enhanced.

Thankfully, though, our police escort never stepped inside the bar. Had they done so, any tolerance for us would have instantly evaporated. The Spanish authorities were ruthless in their opposition to the spread of drugs. Harsh penalties were meted out to people found possessing or pushing drugs, but that didn't stop me.

At a disco one night, I was offered a tablet of LSD. I was a little curious about it, and didn't want to look chicken, so I swallowed the tablet. As the psychedelic drug began bubbling through my bloodstream, I was pitched into a frightening trip.

I sat at a corner table and tried to keep my rebelling senses under control. It was useless. As I gazed around the bar, all the other people—dancing, drinking, talking, laughing—had pigs' heads. They were like characters from a bizarre, comic opera.

More bizarre things began to happen. The walls started to blister and ripple, as they expanded and contracted in time to my breathing. As the night wore on, my mind and imagination continued to turn loops and spirals, and I was thankful when the sensations of sight, sound, and smell began to recede and I was finally able to collapse into bed.

The next morning, the experiences of my acid trip seemed frustratingly close at hand, yet impossible to reach. While I had emerged unscathed, I was too scared and cautious to risk another trip. The story my friends told me of their group experience—when they had seen each other with their heads chopped off, blood gushing from severed arteries—only served to convince me I didn't need LSD. I swore to myself that I would never touch drugs again. Plenty of alcohol and the chance to score with a girl were all I needed, I convinced myself.

But the endless round of heavy drinking, sleeplessness, poor diet, and promiscuous sex were taking their toll on me. I needed something to keep me together. Then I was introduced to "boogaloo."

Amphetamine, speed, uppers—it had a variety of names, but the same effect. After an hour or so, the first four or five tablets would make me buzz. It was as though a generator deep inside began pouring energy into my system. I felt wildly alive, and talked away at supersonic speed, my words accompanied by rapid body movement. The rush of the drugs kept me constantly fidgety. It was uncomfortable to stand for even a moment without hopping from one leg to the other, and I served and carried drinks around the bar at a furious pace.

At midnight it was time to drop some more boogaloo, which kept me scorching until 3:00 a.m. or later, when the final late drinkers were either guided or carried out. By then, I was usually too wide awake and full of energy to consider sleep, so I went into town and met up with some other English workers for more drinks. With so much boogaloo in my system, I felt like King Kong. It pumped me full of all the confidence I lacked when I was sober. I thought I'd discovered what I needed to make my life complete.

On occasion, I was so wired that I wouldn't stop for two or three days at a time—partying, working, more partying, and more working. Even at the end of these stretches, I did little more than collapse on the sand for a couple of hours sleep during the afternoon before starting over. I washed down another handful of boogaloo tablets with a beer or two, then headed out for another night at the Crazy Horse Saloon. And so the cycle went.

Slowly, though, the number of vacationers began to trail off as the temperatures began to cool. The end of the tourist season was approaching. Then one night, after a final drunken celebration at the Crazy Horse Saloon, it was time to pull down the shutters for the last time.

The party was over; the girls were gone. As I packed my bags to return to Nottingham with no job, and little money left from the hundreds of pounds I had earned and stolen during the summer, I wondered for a moment if it had all been worth it. Despite all the girls I had been with, all the good times my friends and I had drunk to, I was going home feeling empty and lost.

In just a few short months, my "paradise" had exacted a heavy toll. My weight had dropped to just over one hundred twelve pounds. My teeth and gums were sore and yellowing. My hair was lank and beginning to fall out, and I was addicted to huge quantities of alcohol and drugs. As my train pulled into the Nottingham station, I thought back to the events that had brought me to this state.

2

Distant Relatives

From an early age, I had known what it was to feel like an outsider. Our house was always the center of much noise, laughter, and high spirits—yet even as a small child, I seemed isolated from it all. Everything seemed to be happening just beyond my grasp. This inability to reach out and be a part of what was going on around me was like a clamp that squeezed me tight on the inside.

My dad, Harry Goodfellow, was a Roman Catholic from Tempo, a small farming community near Enniskillen, Northern Ireland. Despite his capacity for tough labor and a willingness to work hard, Dad had been unable to find regular work. So, like many of his friends before him, he looked "across the water" to where opportunities for hard physical work were plentiful and, by comparison, well rewarded. Dad arrived in England in 1930, and soon found work digging roads for a pipe-laying company in Kent.

Tall, broad, and with a talent for playing the fiddle, Dad quickly became a popular figure among the expatriate groups that gathered most nights to drink to and sing of the beloved homeland they had left behind. It was through one of these Irish nights that Harry, or "Paddy," as he was more commonly known, came to meet a young woman named Bina.

She was from Macroom, Ireland, near Cork. Also a Catholic, Bina had shown her strength of character and independence when, at the age of fifteen, she had run away from home to seek employment in England. As one of eight children, she had a happy childhood, but decided she wanted more out of life. Through contact with an older sister who was already in England, she had been able to find work as a private maid in Sevenoaks.

By the time they were married, Dad had secured a better job working for a brewery. After the wedding, they settled into their first home, a rented apartment, where my older brother, Tony, was born within the first year of their new life together. My sister, Joan, was born seven years after Tony, and three years after that, I arrived, weighing in at just under seven pounds.

By the time I was born, our family had moved to the Midlands town of Nottingham. The industrial heartland of Britain was strong and growing, and Dad had decided to relocate the family after being invited by relatives to go into the business of transporting coal around the region.

The work suited Dad's temperament, combining hard work with personal pride—giving value for money and good, reliable service. The business prospered, and soon our home was a comfortable, well-appointed house with its own garden—a far cry from my parents' early days.

Dad was well liked and respected by customers, colleagues, and friends. He was uncompromising, yet scrupulously fair. He prided himself in caring for his family, but his love for a drink with his friends sometimes left his good intentions unfulfilled.

My parents often argued late into the night about the money Dad wasted on his drinking friends. "What is a man if he can't look after his mates?" he always countered. Then they screamed back and forth. On occasion, they threw more than just accusations and insults at each other—crockery and ornaments crashed against the walls. At those times, I knelt against the banister at the top of the stairs, my eyes squeezed shut, my jaw clenched in the forlorn hope that I could make it all go away.

Their rage seemed to know no limits. On one occasion, Dad, who was always doing improvements around the house, spent hours putting new paneling up the stairwell. Not long afterward, an argument erupted, and in an uncontrolled rage, Dad systematically put his fist through every panel he had put in place only days before.

Sometimes I lay awake at night with dread in my heart. What if Mom really left Dad, as I had so often heard her threaten? I wished the arguments would stop. But somehow their violent disagreements seemed to fuel their relationship, acting as a strange cement for the love they had for each other, but couldn't seem to express in a more tender way.

Although Dad tried to care for us all in practical ways, we never seemed to spend much time together as a family. He either worked long hours, or drank with his friends at one of the local Irish pubs.

I relished the times when Dad arrived home in time for dinner. Together with Tony and Joan, I clambered onto the sofa and begged him to tell us one of his war stories, before he could slip on his jacket to head off for a few beers.

We were spellbound as Dad told us of how he had been in the thick of the fighting in France during the early days of World War II. Under heavy artillery fire, the British infantry had been forced back, and soon the crack German Panzer tank division was pushing through the British line. After blowing up their own guns to keep the Germans from capturing and using them, Dad's unit fell back to the French shores.

During the battle, Dad and his unit came under heavy bombardment, and were pinned down in some woods for three nights. They joked about sending one of their number over to a nearby vineyard to bring back some wine to help pass the time. They drew straws, and Dad pulled the short one.

Instead of the joke it was intended to be, Dad, true to character, took it as a serious pledge. Despite the shells exploding all around, he snaked his way over to the vineyard. Once there, he had to lay low for five hours until the heavy enemy barrage subsided, before making his way back with several trophy bottles of wine tucked securely in his kit bag.

"And you know," he always said, pausing a moment to look at his three wide-eyed children, "I believe that the hand of God was on me then...."

His conviction was born out of what had happened next. Finally arriving at Dunkirk, Dad and his unit found a scene of carnage and chaos. Heavy casualties were being inflicted on the British forces as they were plucked from the beach by an armada of small boats.

Dad and his friends dug foxholes in the sand, awaiting their turn to find space on one of the craft that bobbed up and down as close to the shore as they dared come. Finally their turn came, and the order was given to run for one of the boats. They began their dash across the sand.

As they charged into the water, two of his friends made for the nearest boat, shouting at Dad to follow. There were spaces for eight or nine men on board, and they were the first in line. But something deep inside Dad told him not to head that way. "No, not that one," he screamed, grabbing them by the arms and pulling them back. Instead, they waded across to another, smaller craft in the distance. As they did so, a direct hit shattered the first boat, killing all on board.

Arriving back in Ramsgate on a small liner called *The Daffodil*, Dad, like many of the other fortunate Dunkirk survivors, was allowed home leave. But when he returned for further duty, he had another experience that convinced him there was some divine intervention in his military service.

Dad was to be shipped overseas to Burma, where the British were ensnared in a ferocious battle with the Japanese. Shortly before he was due to leave, a bout of food poisoning hospitalized him for weeks. It was so serious that his stomach was affected for the rest of his life. By the time Dad was well enough to be discharged from the hospital, his unit had already left for Burma. In Burma, during the Battle of Irawodi, his unit suffered massive losses.

These experiences had obviously made a great impact upon him, and he told his story with a mixture of wonder and curiosity. While whiskey raised his passions and added luster to other stories, his wartime memories never altered, whether he was drunk or sober.

Listening to Dad recall his war days made me want to act them out. I took the rifle he had carried on his back at Dunkirk—a long, heavy weapon handed to him by a Belgian cavalryman—and shot imaginary enemies, all the while puzzling over why God, whoever He was, was so interested in my father. It never occurred to me that this God was the same person about whom there was so much fuss made each week.

On Sunday mornings, we were always greeted with the stale smell of beer, whiskey, and cigarette smoke from the night before. Mom struggled to get us all neatly dressed and ready for morning mass, while at the same time making breakfast and organizing lunch. As she busied herself, she complained to Dad about the previous night's party. Dad was invariably nursing a hangover.

Somehow, though, we always managed to squeeze into our best clothes and down our breakfast just in time to march off solemnly to St. Patrick's, the big, square, red brick church at the corner.

Inside it was dark, cold, and very confusing. I was sandwiched in by solemn-faced, weary adults. At regular intervals, they stood or knelt as though they were playing some kind of game. They spoke in indifferent, flat voices, in a language I didn't understand. All I knew was that it was very important to be there. The arguments that ensued to make sure we arrived on time convinced me of that. But I could never work out why it was so important; everyone looked so grim while they were there.

As the service progressed, I squirmed in my seat and peered around at the adults. Their faces were gray and set, as though their minds were a million miles away. Dad reached over and pinched me to stop me from fidgeting, but that only made me more determined to keep on.

At the back of the church hung a picture of Jesus, similar to the ones that hung in our bedrooms at

home. His eyes were mournful, his hands had large
wounds, and there was a lot of blood. Father Saul,
the parish priest, told me that Jesus had died for me.
I found the whole idea rather disturbing. Yet every
time as I turned to walk out of church, Jesus seemed
to glare at me from the picture.

While boring, at least things were calm in church,
and for that reason alone, it was almost enjoyable.
But I always knew that it wouldn't be too long before
Mom and Dad were busy quarreling again. As the
mass drew to a close, everyone rushed for the door.
Outside, the men disappeared into a cloud of cigarette smoke as they lit up in unison.

For the first time in two hours, Dad and his
friends had big smiles on their faces as they sauntered down to the local pub. We headed home with
Mom for lunch. Later, when Dad invariably rolled
home too drunk and too late to eat, there were more
arguments, shouts, and confrontations. Mom threw
Dad's lunch at him, and there were screams and
scuffles, after which Dad fell asleep until dinnertime.

The Sunday of my first communion is the only
Sunday I remember when there wasn't a fight. I was
chosen to carry the banner in the parade of children
receiving their first sacraments, and I was dressed in
white robes and fussed over by relatives. Such an
honor made Mom very proud. Following the service,
there was a party in the church yard, with cakes, tea,
and soda pop laid out on trestle tables.

There was one bright spot on Sundays, though.
After Dad ate his lunch—if it was still edible, or
Mom hadn't thrown it at him or the wall—and slept
off most of his lunchtime drinking, he often took us
to the local cinema. It was a run-down, old movie
theater, but I remember it with great affection, be-

cause it was one of the few places we did something together as a family. Sure, we didn't speak to each other, and it was dark, but as I sat in that flickering atmosphere, with cartoons and feature movies passing before me, I drank in the sense of closeness and contentment of having my family around me. How I wished I could catch that feeling and take it home with me! But as the final credits began rolling and we headed home, reality set in.

Somehow, the good times just seemed to get spoiled. We tried so hard to make Christmas, St. Patrick's Day, and birthdays into family occasions to be enjoyed, but something always went wrong. The day drew to a close, and I felt desperately unhappy, because what had begun with such high hopes had ended in arguments and bitterness.

Even without visitors and guests—of which there was an endless stream—our home was always busy. Yet I felt alone and left out. I shared a bedroom with Tony, but he was ten years older than I, and had little time for a baby brother.

Sometimes at night, I was terrified at the thought that there was a monster lurking beneath my bed, just waiting for the right moment to snake out a tentacle or a scaly hand and drag me off. I called and pleaded with Tony to check under my bed, but he only jeered and told me not to be stupid.

At times, the fear was so heavy that I pulled the sheets up over my head and whispered, "Please, God, don't let them get me." I didn't know who God was, whether He could hear me, or if He was interested in helping me, should He be listening. But I had nowhere else to turn, and in my terror, I clutched for any straw I could find.

I always felt closer to my friends than I did to my family. Although my two sisters were nearer my age, we never seemed to get along. We always fought and argued over who owned something, and whether we were allowed to use it. So instead, I played with my friends in the streets near our house.

Dad's business went sour, and by the time I started high school, we had lost the nice, comfortable house with the garden. Instead, we lived in shabby, rented rooms in a private house on London Road, while Dad tried to get another business started.

London Road was located in one of the worst slum areas of Nottingham. It was directly across from the county football ground, and we always knew when a team had scored by the roar of the crowd that burst through our windows. Our family squeezed into the three upstairs rooms, and shared the bathroom and kitchen with the owner and her son, Keith.

Keith was one of my closest friends, and we ran and played together in the streets. We were always careful, though, never to venture too far from home. The crowded back-to-back houses and alleys were a maze of small communities, and there were only a few streets in our area where it was safe to walk. If you wandered too far afield, you were venturing into someone else's territory, and they didn't always take kindly to the intrusion.

Yet for all the hardship, there was a strong sense of community in this predominantly Irish neighborhood. This sense of national spirit was important to my parents, whose lives seemed to center on weekly gatherings to reminisce about life in Ireland, and to sing the songs they had grown up with.

With conditions for our growing family so cramped, Dad was one of the first to be offered a home in a new public housing project being built in the Woollaton district, a newly created suburb on the other side of Nottingham. When we moved into our new house, work on the project was not completed, so we had to clamber across on planks just to get to our front door.

Despite it being the best-equipped and maintained house in which we had ever lived, my parents couldn't seem to settle down. They missed the local pubs, the bustling sense of neighborliness, the noise, the fights, and the squabbles of the slums. So, after just a few months, we moved back to the slums, this time to the very heart of the notorious Meadows district.

By then, Dad's work fortunes had improved. He had managed to secure a job as a steel erector working on the new power station sites springing up around the region.

These sites were dangerous and demanding places to work. But they suited my father well, and he was soon made foreman, which meant he had to keep the hard-drinking, wild migrant workers in check. It was a job that demanded quick thinking, a quick tongue, and quick fists. And he had all three.

Once, after finding that a scaffolder's shoddy work had put an entire team at risk, Dad fired him. The angry worker, a broad, solid Cockney, came down to the Meadows looking for Dad. He found him in one of his favorite local pubs, and challenged him to a fight. Dad went outside with the man, and laid him out cold on the pavement. When the man came around, Dad took him back into the pub and bought him a beer, and they became good friends.

Dad was earning a good salary, and we were able to rent a large, rambling house in Wilford Grove. From the center of this tree-lined street, you could see Nottingham Castle on the highest point of the hill, a couple of miles away. Dad renovated the house from top to bottom, and in addition to throwing open the doors on weekends for parties, we took in Irish lodgers who worked on various construction sites up and down the Midlands.

Among the tenants in our double-fronted home was a cousin, who came home drunk one night and got into a violent argument with Mom. The argument ended with him attacking Mom and then Tony, who tried to come to her assistance. When Dad came home and found out what had happened, he savagely beat the cousin up and threw him out of the house.

We thought that was the end of the matter until later that evening. With screams and curses, our cousin burst through the front door brandishing a butcher knife. "I'm going to kill you all!" he screamed in a drunken rage. Dad herded us all into the front room, and held the door closed while the cousin ranted and raved on the other side. Then we watched in horror as the knife blade started to break through the thin paneling.

Thankfully, our neighbors, realizing the commotion was more than our usual domestic disputes, called the police. They arrived just in time to disarm our cousin and bundle him away.

Following that incident, Dad redoubled his efforts to teach me how to fight. He showed me how to punch and guard myself, and insisted I repeat the maneuvers until I got them right. He also trained me how to knock someone to the ground with a swift kick at their legs.

"The best way to settle an argument, Johnny," he told me earnestly, "is to get the first punch in. Worry about the talking afterward."

3

Letting Go

Dad's bruising philosophy became the hallmark of my young life. During my second year of school, it exploded in a way that would be repeated, with increasing ferocity, in the years to come.

My first day at school had been fun. Everyone at St. Patrick's, the small grade school attached to the local church, had made a special effort to make us feel welcome, and I really enjoyed it...for the first and last time in my school career. I soon discovered that school was not a bright new world opening before me. I was not suited for the academic life.

Today I might be diagnosed as having a learning disability, but back then, I was merely written off as one who wouldn't go far in school, or life, for that matter. It was never actually said, but I picked it up from the teachers. They put their time and energy into the brighter kids in the class, while my efforts were looked over hurriedly, if at all.

This feeling of being on the outside extended from the classroom into the playground. Despite my regular "lessons" from Dad, I still wasn't confident about getting into a fight. I was smaller than average, and the free-for-all antics on the playground scared me. To make matters worse, the school bully, Mick, seemed to sense my uncertainty and singled me out. Mick was two years older than I and regularly goaded and made fun of me. I longed to lash out and hurt him, but fear of retaliation kept my anger locked inside, where it quietly simmered.

Then, one day, it happened. I had spent many hours during our craft lessons modeling a submarine out of clay. Since I was not academically inclined, I was delighted when I discovered something I was fairly good at. I had painstakingly fashioned my handiwork, all the while looking forward to the time I could take it home and show Mom. Praise for my schoolwork was rare. It would be a real treat.

When my model was finished, I lovingly carried it through the streets toward home. As I rounded a corner, I came face to face with Mick and some of his friends.

"What have you got there, Goodfellow?" Mick demanded.

"Nothing...I was just on my way home."

"You're lying. Come on, let's have a look," and they forced me to reveal my tenderly held treasure. As I lifted it up for them to see, Mick whipped his hand forward and flicked the model from my grasp. My model submarine fell to the pavement, shattering into a dozen pieces. Mick laughed a mean, mocking laugh, while his friends smirked and giggled.

Normally, I would never have considered fighting Mick, but before I knew what was happening, I was screaming at him: "You rotten swine, I'm going to kill you for that!" All my pent-up frustration, loneliness, insecurity, and resentment burst out in a furious rush of emotion.

Mick sneered at me contemptuously, but his expression turned to bewilderment and then alarm as I balled my fists and landed the first punch. Screaming uncontrollably, I began lashing wildly at him. He jumped back, turned, and began to stumble away. As he did, I sensed a rush of excitement within. My unguarded rage had scared him, and had given me the upper hand.

My hands were empty when I finally arrived home that day, but I had discovered something important. If I just let go and gave my feelings free rein to express themselves through my fists and feet, then even the biggest, toughest opponent could be overcome. I wouldn't need to feel intimidated by anyone anymore, if I made sure they had a reason to fear me.

While this revelation made me feel secure in the playground and on the streets around my home, it did nothing to quell the surging tension inside. Arguments and fights at home, emptiness and confusion at church, and inferiority and loneliness at school, all combined to leave my emotions coiled like a spring.

The only time I experienced any inner calm and peace was during the summers, when my mother took us to Ireland to spend time with her relatives. We visited members of the family living in and around Cork, staying in their little thatched cottages, and running freely in the fields and country lanes.

The open space, fresh air, and beautiful countryside was such a contrast to the dirty brick streets of the English Midlands. I spent hours with distant cousins, learning how to trap rabbits, and helping carry huge, packed lunch baskets down to the fields, where the adults were busy bringing in the harvest.

But all too soon, we were back in our big, old house in Wilford Grove, with the weekend parties and the battles at home and in the playground.

My battles at home became more and more vicious. Since Tony was so much older than the rest of us children, he had little to do with us. Joan was three years older than I, and I saw her only as competition. I found myself competing with her over everything; who would be the first to read the weekly comic book, who would sit in the best chair or get a second helping at dinner, but most importantly, who would win our parents' affection. If family closeness was in short supply, then I hated having to share it with anyone else. I wanted to savor every precious ounce of it myself.

We were always looking for ways to outdo each other, and when Mom and Dad weren't looking, our spiteful teasing and tormenting quickly gave way to slaps and punches. As Joan got older, she teased me in front of her friends, pushing me around and trying to humiliate me. I responded by making sure my punches connected hard and painfully whenever we tangled.

By the time Trish was born, I had already started school. Trish was the much-loved baby of the family. We all helped to care for her; I even took my turn at feeding her and changing an occasional diaper. I wasn't good at it, but the responsibility made me feel like a trusted adult.

But as Trish grew up she, too, joined in the competition for Mom's and Dad's affections. As time went by, I found myself clashing with Trish more fiercely than I had with Joan. When Mom and Dad were out, having driven each other to the breaking point, we dove at each other with fists and feet flailing.

By then, I had learned how to trigger my temper almost at will. The results were alarming. I had no qualms about punching and hitting either of my sisters as hard as I could. It made no difference to me that they were girls; they got what they deserved.

But on one occasion, my uncontrolled rage frightened me. I threw Trish against a thick paneled door, laying her out cold. I dragged her into the bedroom, opened the windows, and with the help of the fresh air, managed to bring her around before Mom and Dad got back.

By the time I became aware of my emerging sexuality, my attitude toward women was exemplified in my treatment of Joan and Trish. I was confused. My behavior toward woman was flawed, and most of my education about sex was of the crude playground variety.

There was a strange sense of disgust mixed with exhilarating excitement that pulsed through me the first time I went "all the way" with a girl. I told my parents I was going over to a friend's house for a while. It wasn't a lie, really; but it wasn't the full truth, either.

Rosy was a sort of friend, though if the truth were known, I wasn't interested in her as a person at all. All Rosy was to me was a body—a body that fed my growing fascination with sex.

I wondered, as I wound my way through the streets to her house, what her parents would think if they knew what she was going to do in their bedroom while they were out. But mostly, I didn't care. My thoughts were frozen—subordinated to fulfilling my schoolboy fantasies.

The feelings that surged through me were more electric and hypnotic than the feelings I had experienced leering over men's magazines with my friends. Yet at the same time, a deep sense of self-loathing pulled at me to turn around and walk away.

But the urges I was feeling inside kept drawing me like a magnet toward Rosy's.

Even as I knocked at her door, trying to look relaxed and calm, I knew that the sensory overload I would experience in the following couple of hours would be followed by a flood of guilt and shame, but I was powerless to help myself.

Fantasies and thoughts about sexual activity dominated my life. My days and nights were swamped with thoughts of what I would like to do with a woman. At Rosy's that day, my thoughts and fantasies spilled into action. My mind whirled with the feelings.

Later that night, I crept up to my bedroom, and hoped Mom was asleep; I couldn't have stood to look her in the eyes. I was certain she would know the dreadful thing I had done. Fortunately, she was asleep, and I collapsed onto my bed, feeling hollow and empty. The excitement of having fulfilled my fantasies had been short-lived, and I wondered if I hadn't set a tiger free inside that would turn and devour me. I fell into a fitful sleep.

Those earliest sexual experiences severed the last fragile threads that held me to the church.

For two years, I had served as an altar boy at St. Patrick's. My understanding of God—or, rather, my lack of it—hadn't changed. God seemed no more than a vague and guilty idea in some people's minds. But my serving at the altar not only thrilled my parents (there was a certain amount of social status that came with having your child serve in such a position), but also helped the ordeal of Sunday morning to pass more quickly. I figured that if I had to go to church, I might as well have something to do to help the minutes pass more quickly.

So each Sunday morning, I joined several other

boys who also served at the altar. We fought over who got to wear the cleanest robes—the white linen shirt with a long, black cassock over the top. We put on our most angelic, innocent-looking faces, with our hair close-cropped and slicked down, as we solemnly stood at the front of the church and assisted Father Saul with the mass.

Within a few weeks of starting to experiment with sex, I began to dread serving at church. I wondered if Father Saul could read my mind every time he looked at me with his gentle, caring eyes. I was horrified at the prospect that he might know I had let him down.

If that thought wasn't terrible enough, attending Saturday evening confession with Dad was excruciating. Waiting to enter the small, screened box, which always smelled of whiskey and perfume, my hands started sweating profusely, and I wiped them repeatedly on the sides of my pants.

Once inside the booth, I felt compelled to confess all I had done. My cheeks burned with shame as I recounted everything. I hated having to admit the things my uncontrolled desire had made me do. I always left confession feeling horribly exposed, wondering if the priest had recognized my voice, even though I had tried to disguise it, and would tell my family all I had done.

But sex wasn't my only area of experimentation. Eager to grow up and leave behind the schoolboy image, my friends and I began to dabble in other activities that we believed were a sign of maturity beyond our years.

If we all contributed a few pennies each, we were able to scrape together enough money to buy a pack of Woodbines. They were plain, rough cigarettes, and their smoke roared against the back of our throats, making our eyes water and sting as we inhaled. The first few times I tried smoking, it took all the strength I could muster to keep myself from throwing up on the spot.

But as time went by, the level of unpleasantness began to subside. I found myself looking forward to the next cigarette, and soon my liking for nicotine had developed into a craving. Soon, most of my money was going toward the cost of my next pack of cigarettes.

Alcohol had always flowed in our home as naturally as tea or coffee. My parents never objected to me having a few sips from their glass, if we were awake during one of their late night parties. Soon, though, my friends and I started smuggling bottles of beer away from our parents' supplies and drinking them secretly. I quickly acquired the stomach for alcohol, and the taste for it followed soon after.

All this rebellious activity fueled my hatred of authority, which I saw personified in anyone connected with school. I loathed every passing minute of my time at high school.

We argued back and forth at home as to whether I should be allowed to attend Trent Bridge Boys' School. All my closest friends were going to go there, and I wanted to go, as well.

Tucked away at the edge of the Meadows, just a few hundred yards from the River Trent, Trent Bridge Boys' School had the reputation of being one of the toughest schools in town. But it was a Protestant establishment, which aroused much suspicion in my family. Finally, though, Mom and Dad relented and allowed me to go. On my first day, I discovered just why it had such a tough reputation.

In grade school, my rage had served me well. Not only was I able to fight when I had to, but the sheer ferocity of my rage, earned me respect among the other students. At high school, I found myself once more at the bottom of the pecking order. The boys in the upper grades were determined to make sure we new students knew our place.

Before and after school, the bigger boys picked us off one at a time for a brisk roughing up. Their favorite tortures were to bend our arms behind our backs and stretch them agonizingly over the metal railing, or for two or more of them to hold us still while another burned the sides of our necks with a lit cigarette.

I hated the feeling of helplessness I experienced in the face of these bullies. I despised them for making me aware of my insecurity.

Then, one day, while we were away on a school field trip, the older boys' leader singled me out for special attention. He began taunting and cursing me. Then he pushed me away from the group that had gathered to watch my humiliation.

"Go on, Goodfellow, get lost before we beat you up good and proper!" he hissed.

Somewhere, deep inside, something snapped, and I exploded in a fit of rage. I lunged at him, grabbing his arms and throwing him over my hip, as Dad had taught me during our "lessons" in the front room at home.

As he crashed to the ground, I dropped on top of him, straddling him and pinning him. With methodical and cool satisfaction, I began to pound his face with my fists. I plowed one fist into one side of his face and, as I drew it back, crunched the other fist into the other side. I continued my onslaught with delight, until I was finally dragged off by several of the other boys.

It turned out to be one of the worst things I could

have done. All the older boys felt slighted that a younger student had got the better of one of their classmates. They seemed to think that they each had to take me on to prove their own toughness. From then on, I was constantly trying to avoid unnecessary confrontations. On one occasion, though, I wasn't fast enough on my feet, and ended up being cornered and "branded" with a cigarette by a group of older boys.

The pain didn't enrage me, though it hurt and took time for my singed flesh to heal. The shame and humiliation I experienced, however, did enrage me. It tore at my insides. I couldn't disguise the blistered reminder of the attack on the side of my neck, and I seethed against those who had left me with such a visible mark of defeat.

Dad didn't seem to mind all the fights I got into at school. Instead, when I arrived home from school with skinned knuckles or a bruised cheek, he seemed more interested in a blow-by-blow account of the action than in my injuries. Sometimes I was proud of the way I had handled myself in a situation, and was glad to relay the details to him. Most often, though, I just wished he would express some concern or tenderness for me. I wanted love and affection, not tips on how to handle myself better next time.

Throughout my time at high school, I continued to be plagued by my inability to absorb information. However, my love of reading managed to keep me in the so-called "A-stream" of academic life—barely. Most of the teachers had little time for me, their general attitude being that I would never amount to anything. "You'll probably end up in prison, Goodfellow," one of them flatly told me one day.

The staff's lack of interest in me, coupled with their positions of authority, made them prime targets for my fierce hatred. I daydreamed about getting back at them, especially after being punished. Each teacher had their preferred method of punishment. Some used leather straps, others used bamboo canes or wooden rulers. One teacher insisted that we hold our hand out, palm up, while he administered stinging strokes with a leather strap. If we pulled our hand away, which was the immediate reaction to the pain, he simply doubled the dosage. With every stroke of punishment, my rage grew.

My clash with authority came to a head during a metal working class in my last year at high school. The teacher's name was Marcisniak; he was a squat, muscular Pole who had come to Britain during the war, and stayed on after it was over. He usually ignored me, but on this particular day, he came over to see how I was getting along with my project. I had been trying to make a brass bowl, but I hadn't done a very good job of beating out the shape, although I'd tried hard.

Marcisniak barraged me with criticism about my work. He told me I was doing it all wrong, and would have to start over and do it right. "Concentrate this time. Don't be an idiot all your life, boy!" he snapped.

Being picked on for failing to do the job right, despite my best efforts, was bad enough in front of a classroom full of my friends. But to be ridiculed in front of them was too much.

"Don't call me an idiot!" I shot back.

Marcisniak reached over and slapped me hard on the top of the head. The next thing I knew, I was on top of him, wrestling him onto the workbench. He screamed and kicked as I tried to land one really good punch in his face, but he was too powerful for me, and finally managed to subdue me with the help of another staff member who had rushed in to see what all the commotion was about.

I was hauled in front of the principal, where I was given a verbal dressing-down and threatened with immediate expulsion from school. I didn't really care if I was thrown out, and argued that Marcisniak had started it all because he had struck me first, and that there was a classroom of witnesses—my friends—who had seen it happen.

The episode soon blew over, but it made me more determined than ever to leave school as soon as I could.

That day finally arrived, and on our last day of school, we departing fifteen-year-olds were gathered together by the principal. It was time for his fatherly pep talk about going out into the big, wide world and making our way as young men with the future before us. I looked at him as he droned on, and mused with delight that I would never have to see his smug face again as long as I lived. Walking through the school gates that afternoon for the last time was like being released from prison. I was finally free!

"This is it," I thought, as I walked home. "I've finally made it. No more 'Yes, sir. No, sir.' No more people stopping me from doing what I want to. From now on, people had just better make sure they don't get in my way!"

4

Squaring Up

Despite my academic failings, I managed to secure a job as a trainee inspector at a small factory on the other side of town. It soon became apparent, though, that I was once again a little fish in a big pond. I hated being the butt of the older men's jokes and taunts, and being singled out as "the new kid."

My supervisors soon realized, too, that I wasn't capable of grasping everything that an inspector needed to know in a factory that turned out brass rings by the thousands. After a few weeks on the job, I was put to work on a capstan lathe.

I was embarrassed and humiliated, sure that everyone knew I wasn't up to the job I had originally been given. In reality, most of them didn't even know my name, and cared little about what I was doing.

Then it became obvious that even the sequences of lathe operations were too much for me, and I found myself being handed a plain brown overcoat and a broom. I was now at the bottom of the pile, reduced to sweeping the floors, moving heavy loads of metal from one end of the factory floor to the other, and brewing tea.

This rapid demotion confirmed my worst fears. I felt stupid, worthless, and despised. To make matters worse, there was no one I could turn to: I couldn't bring myself to tell my parents. They still thought I was a trainee-inspector, and I passed over the occasional questions about how things were going at work with a deliberately vague answer, or attempted to change the topic. I couldn't bring myself to admit that I had failed, and I feared my father's scorn at not having "made the grade."

For a year, I quietly endured the job, spending my time daydreaming about sex, or how I would like to get back at all the people who had put me down. I wove violent fantasies of revenge and lust that somehow only managed to make the mundane reality around me even more infuriating.

I eventually quit, convincing Mom and Dad that I had left because there were no prospects for advancement in such a small company for someone with as much talent as I.

It was a couple of months before I managed to find a new job. I considered the idea of following in my brother Tony's footsteps and becoming a miner. I knew that life underground could be dangerous—Tony was off work for the better part of a year one time, recovering from a cave-in that had damaged his back. But I still fancied the idea of being a miner, that is, until I went down into a mine for a visit. The heat, dirt, and darkness hundreds of feet below ground were alarming. Any romantic notions of attacking black seams of coal with a pick were left behind on my way back up to the surface.

Then one day, I decided to try bricklaying. I was apprenticed to a local firm, Costain and Sons, who had contracts to build on the big city center develop-

ment sites in Nottingham. I soon discovered that I'd
found something I was good at. In a strange way, I
felt free for the first time I could recall.

There is an art to laying bricks well. It all has to
do with feel and touch, so gloves are out. After a few
weeks, my fingers toughened up and got used to the
cold. Sometimes, the temperature dropped so low
that I had to spend the first few minutes of the day
chipping ice off the bricks that had been left out
overnight.

The building sites were a man's world—rough
and tough—and it felt good to be accepted as "one
of the guys." We shared coarse jokes, and guffawed
at young girls as they blushed and hurried away.

I enjoyed the sense of achievement and satisfaction that bricklaying brought me. It was something
that had eluded me in all my days of struggling with
books and pens at school. I was adept at "rolling the
board"—taking fresh cement and slapping it down
on top of a row of bricks so that it spread along a
couple of feet. Then I smeared it flat, so the next row
of bricks were level as they were placed carefully
and firmly on top. Next was "buttering the edge"—
running a smear of cement over the side of each brick
to be laid, so that it would be mortared to the brick
next to it.

I was told when I started work that a good bricklayer could lay a thousand bricks a day, and it wasn't
long before I was up to that mark. As a result, my
work was appreciated, and I was given the best jobs.
I pushed myself hard in order to keep the top spot I
had earned. At last I was someone!

The long hours of climbing, stretching, and carrying wound a steely thread into my body, and I
relished the newfound sense of power and strength.
I was stronger and fitter than I had ever been, and

that awareness heightened my readiness to throw a punch or two. I was not someone to be tangled with lightly.

The men on the building sites were a good bunch to work with—they were like family in a strange way. We swore, fought, and tried to outdo each other, but there was a feeling of all being in it together. I liked the feeling of being a part of something.

My employers spotted my natural talent for bricklaying, and teamed me with one of their most experienced men, who responded warmly to me. We worked long and hard together.

My apprenticeship in bricklaying consisted of four years of on-the-job training, as well as some training courses at a local technical college. At the end, I would receive a City and Guild's Certificate in Bricklaying.

While I had a natural talent for bricklaying, and got much satisfaction from working hard on the job, my sense of inadequacy seemed to be compounded every time I walked into the classroom for one of my courses. Finally, after eighteen months, the technical college expelled me for being too rebellious and argumentative—which included a study room brawl with another young apprentice who had dared to criticize my practical work.

Because my bricklaying abilities won me the respect of the older men on the job, I was spared much of the treatment meted out to newcomers. There was a definite pecking order on the building site, and everyone had their place. They were kept there with threats, abuse, and, when needed, violence.

Many of the men on the work crews were fresh out of prison, and they brought an extra sense of aggression and anger to the arguments that often took place. "You learn 'inside' never to back down to anyone," one of them told me one day.

The problem was that the carpenters thought they were better than us bricklayers, that somehow their skills were more artistic. It was an unspoken snobbery that occasionally spilled over into words and violence—such as my tangle with Dave.

Dave and I had worked well enough together up to that point. I was helping him move his heavy bag of tools up to the second floor level at a city center building site when the trouble began. Dave had to climb down to get some more materials, leaving me to hold his tool bag until he returned. But even my toughened arms couldn't hold the weight indefinitely. My grip began to slacken, and as it did, some of the tools slipped out the side of the bag and tumbled to the ground, crashing into a pile of bricks as they landed.

Dave saw the accident and shouted up at me angrily, "Can't you do anything right, you weakling? I only asked you to hold my bag for a couple of minutes. What a pathetic excuse for a bricklayer you are!"

His taunt was like a red flag to a bull, and I snapped back, "Who do you think you're talking to, you fat slob?" Peering down at him from above, I felt relatively safe. But as a crowd gathered, I realized I was going to have to defend my honor. I scurried down the ladder and, without waiting for the usual round of curses, taunts, and accusations that precede a fight, I let loose at Dave.

My three left jabs smashed into Dave's face before he knew it. Another series of blows followed, but I hoped someone would step in and break up the fight. If they didn't, I was in trouble.

My body was as hard as my heart, but Dave was

more than a match. He towered four inches above me, and was fifty pounds heavier. I knew that in picking a fight with him, I was asking for trouble, but the risk of physical injury mattered less to me than losing face in front of my fellow workers.

Dave was taken completely by surprise. Thankfully, though, my gamble paid off. Before Dave had a chance to gather his senses and come back at me, some of the onlookers stepped in and pulled me away. Another couple grabbed Dave, and began to calm him down and defuse the situation.

I had fought because I was determined not to lose the sense of identity I had discovered since starting work on the building site. People recognized my abilities and respected my character, and I was prepared to do anything I had to in order not to lose the sense of personal worth and value that recognition had brought me. I would not allow people—of any size—to belittle or taunt me in front of others.

The high regard in which I was held on the job brought me my father's admiration for the first time. However, he showed it in a strange way. Perhaps it was because of the way he had to keep the young men on his construction crews in line, but whatever the reason, he turned to fighting.

There had been many scuffles and tussles at home in the past, and the prospects for a real battle had simmered for a long time. After I'd been at work for several months, I decided that Mom and Dad couldn't make me go with them to church on Sunday mornings any more. So, when Dad's voice came roaring up the stairs, telling me to get up and get dressed, I ignored him, rolled over, and went back to sleep.

Minutes later he thundered up the stairs, crashed

through my bedroom door, and barked at me: "Johnny, I just told you to get up. It's almost time for church, and we are not going to be late, by God...!" I peeked over the top of the sheets and told him flatly: "I'm not going any more, Dad."

"You what?" he exploded, "Don't you think you can tell me what you are and aren't going to do...just get yourself downstairs right away!" With that, he stormed downstairs again. I continued to lie there, tensing myself for another confrontation, until a few minutes later I heard the front door slam shut as Mom and Dad and the girls set off for St. Patrick's without me.

Dad and I never talked about the confrontation again, but he always glared at me at lunchtime on Sundays, when I finally surfaced after a long sleep-in. Not only did my staying home on Sunday mornings bring welcome relief from the insufferable boredom and choking guilt of attending church, but it also brought me a feeling of strength. I had stood up to Dad, and he had backed down. It marked the end of his total domination over me.

Dad was aware of the shift in our relationship, and he began to try and provoke me into a full-scale fight, especially on the nights when he'd had a little too much to drink. "Come on, Johnny, my lad, let's see what you're made of!" he taunted, inviting me forward with a wave of his left hand, while his right was balled up at his chin in a boxer's stance.

Usually I just walked away, or waved him off, saying: "Oh, come on, I don't want to fight you, Dad. That's stupid...."

One night, though, he continued to bait me. "Are you frightened of me or something?" he asked. I didn't get a chance to answer. The next thing I knew, my head exploded in a galaxy of bright stars, and I was lying on my back across the kitchen table. Dad had sent me sprawling with a right hook to my chin.

I flew to my feet with a scream. In a burst of raw anger, I grabbed Dad by the lapels and slammed him backward against the wall, almost lifting him off his feet. Then I threw him down into a chair, bent his head back, and snarled into his face: "If you ever do that again, I'll kill you!"

I meant it, and Dad knew it. All the anger, hurt, and bitterness I had stored up over the years was present in my simple threat. For a brief moment, there was a flicker of uncertainty, perhaps even fear, in Dad's eyes.

It was a sweet moment of bitterness.

5

Easy Money

I earned a good salary as a bricklayer. Working hard to keep up my thousand bricks a day meant that the small brown envelope that was slapped into my waiting palm every Thursday was always satisfyingly full. I usually had plenty of money to throw around on the weekend.

By then, alcohol was an integral part of my life. I paced myself by the hard-drinking habits of the older men around me, and could match their consumption beer for beer. There was always a mug or two of beer at lunch time, and a few more each night down at the local pub. But it was on the weekend that the serious socializing began.

On Friday evenings, I gulped down my dinner, washed and changed, and left the house early. I strolled down to the local pub to have a couple of beers with the neighbors, then straightened my tie and sauntered on into town to one of the busy bars near the city center.

The Flying Horse was a favorite of mine. It always seemed to be packed with more people and noise than the room could easily hold. I swapped stories with my friends about all that had happened during the week, and discussed the prospects of the female company we would find at the dance hall later on.

After leaving the Flying Horse, we drifted on to Yates' Wine Lodge, a place for serious drinking. With its sawdust-covered floor, large mirrored walls, and cast iron ceiling poles, it resembled the deck of a ship stripped bare and tied down before a storm. And that wasn't too far from the truth.

As the alcohol loosened tongues and fists, a storm of fights broke out. We stood in a circle in the center of the room, downing drink after drink, daring anyone to even consider pushing through us on their way to the bar.

Finally, we pressed on to the Locarno or one of the other big dance halls in the city. They were cavernous places with wall-to-wall bars and large dance floors, where girls shuffled in time to the strains of the resident band, just waiting to be picked up by any one of the leering men standing at the sides, eyeing the talent.

Not surprisingly, this kind of living soon ate into my wage packet. My gambling on weeknights at the pubs in the Meadows, coupled with my drinking and dancing appetite, meant my money never lasted through the whole week. I was usually lucky if it lasted for two or three days.

I had already turned to crime as a way of supplementing my income, and felt no guilt about it. One of the easiest ways to make some extra money was at the dance hall.

A friend and I chose a couple of girls and got them talking. When they slipped off to dance—they always went in pairs, giggling—we rifled through their handbags and took out the change purses. We slipped into the men's rest room, where we took out any money and dumped the rest in the toilet. Then we disappeared to another part of the cavernous, crowded club. We reasoned that if we couldn't get the girl into bed, at least we would get her money.

It seemed to me that other people generally had more money than they needed, and I didn't have enough. It was as simple as that—and I also savored the notion of getting something for nothing. It was as though I were getting back at a world that was so set against me.

When stealing and violence could be combined, it was even more satisfying. On one occasion, a friend of mine, Bob, and I were drinking at a shabby Meadow's pub. We were down to our last beer, and payday was still a long way away. I suggested we drink down the last of our beer and go out and find money for the next one—at someone else's expense.

We shuffled into the shadows of an alley a few streets away, within shouting distance of my home. All we could hear was our own shallow breathing as we waited, straining to catch the sound of an approaching step.

Then there was a cough, a shuffle—someone was coming. It sounded like a man, probably on his way home from a quiet drink down at the local pub with his friends. His pockets, we reasoned, would have a few pounds in them.

Half-nervous and half-elated at the audacity of our plan, we waited until the last moment before springing out of the shadows. "You! Give us your money, or there's going to be trouble," we demanded.

Then I heard a crack—the man had given Bob a blow to the face. Things were going wrong. The fear of being identified gripped us, and we redoubled our efforts. The man crumpled to the pavement under our combined attack.

He screamed and shouted for help, and I expected half the neighborhood to come running from their houses. "Shut up, man!" I snarled at him, kicking him in the face with the toe of my boot. He fell silent and curled into a ball, cradling his battered face.

I jerked him onto his side and rifled through his pockets. There wasn't much in them, but we grabbed what little there was and ran. Only after we had run several blocks did we stop to count our pickings. Two pounds. Just enough for a few drinks each.

We heard an ambulance siren as we sauntered back into the pub we had left a half hour before. We leaned over the bar and ordered two pints of the best bitter ale, laughing to each other as we did so. The ale was good, and we savored every drop.

"What do you mean, 'is everything all right?'" I asked one of the old men in the pub, who had wandered over to talk to us. I followed his gaze to the fresh splotches of blood clearly visible on the front of my trousers.

"Oh, that's nothing. We just ran into a little trouble down the road, didn't we, Bob?"

"Yeah, that's right. Just a little trouble. But we sorted it out all right, didn't we, Johnny?" Bob pitched in.

"Yeah. Cheers!"

The old man smiled, turned, and walked away, satisfied with our answer. We smirked to ourselves through the foamy head of the ale.

One Friday night, I slipped out of the Locarno a little after 2:00 a.m., with only a handful of small change in my pocket, and no option but to walk the five miles home. The music and drink still hummed in my veins as I strolled drunkenly through the main shopping area. I looked in all the window displays as I walked, feeling sorry for myself that I didn't have enough money to spend in any of them.

I can't even afford a coat, I moaned to myself as I pulled my thin jacket close in an effort to keep out the early morning chill.

As I wove my way past the large jewelry store on the corner, my mental gears began to whir. An array of rings, brooches, and watches twinkled at me from brightly lit display cases. Before I thought about what I was doing, I ran to a road work site nearby, grabbed a heavy red marker lamp and began to pound the metal case of the lamp against the thick glass window of the jewelry store.

I swung with all my might two, three times. Then, with my fourth swing, the glass shattered. I quickly discarded the lamp and jumped through the window into the display area. I ignored the shrill alarm that had begun shrieking as soon as the glass gave way. I began stuffing my pockets full of everything I could grab.

Rings, tie pins, watches, earrings, bracelets, brooches, necklaces, they were all scooped up frantically as I tore items from display trays and scattered others aside to grab what I wanted. Excitement filled me as I snatched up the jewelry, knowing it was mine for the taking.

With my two jacket pockets bulging, chains trailing over the top, I grabbed a handful of other display cards to my chest, jumped out the window, turned right, and headed up a side street. As I ran, trinkets dropping to the ground all around, a roaring laugh of pleasure broke from my throat. It was such a marvelous feeling! My previous crimes seemed tame by comparison. I was already planning my next break-in.

But the moment was short-lived. I hadn't gotten more than two hundred yards when I heard the unmistakable siren of a police patrol van behind me, pulling to a halt outside the jewelry store. Then panic struck.

"He went that way...there he is!" a man yelled at the police. Adrenalin pumped into my heart, and I began sprinting to the top of the street. I ran around a low wall and into the wide churchyard of St. Nicholas.

My elation gave way to cold, hard fear as I crouched behind a large black tombstone, my heart beating wildly inside my chest. It had all happened too quickly. How had the police managed to arrive at the scene so fast? They had ruined my moment!

As I gasped for breath, I threw the display cards away over the tombstones, where they scattered and rolled.

In a half-crouched position, I peered around the side of the tombstone. Thankfully, there were no street lights close by, so I was in the shadows. I could just make out the police van pulling to a halt at the side of the road, the officer in the passenger seat staring out through the side window with intense concentration.

Careful to keep a low profile, I scurried away behind the tombstones and monuments to another wall at the rear of the church. I'd scaled the wall and made my way to the top of a steep drop of steps that led to a street forty feet below—and probable safety—when I heard dogs barking and a cry.

"There he is! Hey, you, stop. This is the police!"

The shout alarmed me, and as I turned, I lost my footing and tumbled down the steps, cracking my head and ripping my clothes as I went. But fear was an anesthetic. At the bottom, I picked myself up without stopping to think about the bruises, and lunged off through an alley and out into another main street.

At first I thought I'd managed to lose them, but three hundred yards up the street, I heard another shout from behind.

"Hey, you, stop—or we'll let the dogs go!"

I slowed to a halt, my chest heaving from the chase. I knew it was pointless to try to outrun police dogs, so I turned to face my pursuers. The physical exertion of the chase had washed some of the alcohol out of my system, and I was already thinking fairly clearly. What had I done? What was going to happen to me? I had never been caught before. What would my parents say? How could I face people again, once they found out?

The two policemen didn't appreciate the chase I had led them on. The one in front pushed me hard in the chest, backing me up against the wall of an office complex. "You stupid kid, what the hell do you think you've been doing, eh? You've really gone and landed yourself in it for this, I'm telling you!"

He spun me around and pushed my face up against the rough brick wall while he pulled my arms behind me and clicked the handcuffs into place. "You didn't really think you were going to get away with it, did you? You've gone and made things worse for yourself, that's all."

Still swearing angrily at me, they dragged me to their van and threw me into the back, where I was separated from the dogs by only a wire partition.

Throughout the bumpy journey to the police station, the Alsatians barked and snarled at me through the wire. Fear of the dogs, and anger at myself and the police, drove me to smash my fists repeatedly against the inner wall behind the driver's head.

"Let me out of here, you pigs!" I screamed. "I hate you coppers, I hate you!"

I was bundled roughly out of the van and man-handled though the booking process. Then it was down into one of the filthy cells beneath Nottingham's Guild Hall. With a parting warning that they'd remember my face and that I had better watch my back in the future, the policemen slammed the door shut and left me in the dark.

Trapped by my own rage, I pounded on the wall a couple of times with my hands before throwing myself full-length onto the bunk. Covered with only a thin, old blanket, I fell into a heavy, despairing sleep.

A stale, foul smell stole into my nostrils and slid down to the back of my throat, where it seemed to curl into a ball and threatened to make me gag. I wished I didn't recognize it.

I opened one eye a fraction to investigate, being careful not to allow too much harsh light to spill through. It felt as though I had been through a blender, and too much brightness would have started me retching.

Across from where I lay, I could make out a plain, gray wall, and as I looked up, I saw the source of my nausea. Smeared from left to right as far as I could see was dark human excrement. I groaned and clenched my teeth in an attempt to stop my stomach from rebelling against this revolting start to the day.

My sluggish efforts to piece together just where

I was and what I was doing there were abruptly halted as the light seemed to fade. A large shape thrust itself into my face, and I gradually made out the form of a human head. Rancid breath blew into my face as the unshaven, sweaty countenance peered at me.

"What have they got you in for?" the voice demanded in a flat tone.

The question brought bits and pieces of information tumbling into place. This man was sharing the cell into which I had been pitched the previous night after my abortive attempt to escape from the police. The realization only added to the feeling of sickness deep inside.

"Uh, theft...they caught me breaking into a jewelry store downtown...how about you?"

"Rape."

Shocked, I sat up and backed against the wall at the side of the bunk, trying not to show any alarm. It would be far better if he thought I was a regular—rough and tough and used to looking after myself behind bars.

I was saved from having to make any further conversation by the rattling of the heavy iron door set in the far wall. It swung open slowly, and a short-sleeved policeman stepped through to set a mug of tea down on a small, scratched table before giving me a disinterested look and disappearing. The thick door swung closed with an air of finality. I sipped the warm, weak tea and ran my fingers through my untidy hair.

My previously smart blue suit was crumpled, creased, and torn. My mouth felt as though maggots had slept in it, and my stomach pitched and rolled like a cork on a stormy sea. A gagging aroma clung to my clothes and hair. So this was how my high living Friday night had ended!

I had just finished sipping the tea when another policeman opened the door and stuck his head in.

"Goodfellow, come on out. Your old man's here for you upstairs."

I followed him uncertainly. I was dirty, uncomfortable, and hungry. I hoped that Dad had straightened things out and was going to take me home. I discovered the reason for his visit as soon as I stepped into the small interview room at the top of the stairs.

Dad lunged at me from the other side of the room, throwing one punch after another. "What on earth do you think you've been up to, boy?" he demanded. "I never brought you up to become a thief, did I? Is that all you can think of to repay your poor mother after all these years?"

He continued to rant and rave as three policemen pulled him away and sat him down in a chair, urging him to be calm and to collect his thoughts. He looked up at me with anger and shame in his eyes—and then he crumpled. Falling forward and dropping his head into his hands, he began to weep. "Oh, son! Oh, son!" he cried.

I stood against the opposite wall, looking down at the ground and squirming inside. I didn't feel sorry for him, I just felt horribly embarrassed. I didn't know which was worse—that my dad should try to beat me up instead of wanting to take me home, or that he'd burst into tears.

It was another three days before the police let me out on bail—three days in which I grew accustomed to the stench and dirtiness of the place. But I never managed to come to terms with the sense of grievance I felt. It never occurred to me that I had gotten the just deserts for my criminal actions. I just felt sick that the police had caught me.

Going home was agonizing. Dad shouted and swore again, and Mom burst into tears and wrung her hands. The scene was repeated after my appearance at the magistrate's court a few weeks later, where I was fined, ordered to pay costs, and given a two-year suspended prison sentence. It was all reported in the newspaper for our neighbors to see.

For a while, this encounter with the law brought me to my senses. I restricted myself to one or two trips a week to the local pub, where I played cards or dominoes with the older men. Soon, though, I began slipping back into my old ways. Once again, the money I was earning legitimately wasn't enough. But this time around, I stuck to crimes where I was less likely to get caught.

Cars were one of my favorite targets. It was easy, walking along a street late at night, to casually try the handles of the vehicles parked along the way. I was always amazed at how many open doors I found. I rummaged around inside the car and ran off with a coat, cassette player, or perhaps some tools. I sold these to my friends, no questions asked.

Late one evening, I went spying to check on some cars in a temporary parking lot on a derelict site at the back of the town center. In the rear of one of them, I spotted a pile of brand new jeans. I guessed that the driver must have been a traveling salesman, and that the jeans were his samples. None of the car doors were open, but with the help of a brick, I soon shattered the rear window and carried the jeans off in a conveniently left suitcase.

By this time, it was nearly 3:00 a.m., and I headed off toward the train station with my booty in tow. On my way, I encountered a policeman strolling along the empty street. Thinking quickly, so as to avoid suspicion, I went over to him and inquired about the next train to Derby. My forwardness seemed to disarm him, even if it was strange for a young man in a smart blue suit to be carrying a bulging suitcase down an empty street in the early hours of the morning.

"Oh, it leaves about six," he told me brightly.

"Thanks, officer. I'll go in and wait," I replied with a friendly nod.

That was what I did. I went in, napped for a couple of hours, and then caught the train to Derby, the nearest industrial town of any size. Once in Derby, I headed for the building sites, where I knew I could get rid of the jeans, no questions asked. Within three hours, I had sold my entire stock, and even the suitcase. I returned to Nottingham, my hands empty and my wallet bulging.

I sat in the carriage as the train rumbled back toward Nottingham, with a great sense of pride at my accomplishment. I looked at the people seated around me—a young mother, a schoolboy, an executive, and assorted workers—and I wanted to laugh at them for their safe, respectable suburban lives. If they only knew what I had been up to.

6

On the Edge

I enjoyed drinking, and a fight always seemed the perfect way to end an evening. I needed more excitement and stimulation than the average person trapped in the boring nine-to-five world. So, when an old friend called one day to ask if I would like to join the steeplejack trade, I jumped at the opportunity. I would get paid a lot more money for doing the same job as a bricklayer—only up high.

The company I joined had contracts for the repair and maintenance on industrial chimneys all over the Midlands. They were big, red-brick fingers that poked eighty to two hundred feet into the air.

The job was fantastic. It provided the excitement I craved, and kept my emotions charged throughout the day. I was apprenticed to Ted, one of the most experienced steeplejacks in the business, and soon he had me shinnying up and down the sides of chimneys as though I'd been doing it all my life. It was my job to run up and down, bringing Ted his tools and the ten-foot lengths of ladder that he needed to lay a climbing route up the side of the chimney.

Ted climbed halfway up the highest section of ladder, then turned and balanced with his back pressed hard against the rungs. He reached down and took the next section of ladder from me. Once he had it in his grip, he swung his arms over his head and hooked it up to the previous section of ladder. It took ice-cool nerves and cat-like balance, and Ted had a way of making it look as easy as hanging out the laundry to dry. I loved his casual style, and relished getting to the top myself.

Our job was to replace worn and damaged brickwork at the top of the chimney. Once we worked our way to the top, we rigged up a hanging platform for us to sit beside the top of the chimney. Then we knocked away the damaged bricks.

After that came the most crucial part of the operation: removing the steel band that held the chimney together at the top. Even the most experienced steeplejack took a deep breath before undertaking this part of the job. You were never sure how much tension would be released when the metal band was cut: if it was a lot of pressure, it had the potential to flick back and pitch you off your small seat.

There were a number of accidents involving other men in the company during the months I worked with Ted. One steeplejack was hurt when he slipped from a section of ladder that hadn't been properly secured, and another was killed when he toppled from the highest point of a factory chimney.

But such reports didn't deter me. They just reemphasized the danger of what I was doing. At the pub, I told my friends about these incidents as a way of endorsing my bravery and care-free attitude. Until one day....

We were working on an eighty-foot chimney at a hospital. When we reached the top, we discovered that the chimney was still in use, and we could see the warm air shimmering out of the top as we got level with it—a sight every steeplejack hates. Because of the width of the hole at the top, I could only secure the bosun's chair—which would hang from chains stretched across the opening—by inching around the narrow lip of the chimney to the other side.

Sitting astride the lip, I began to scoot my way carefully around to the other side. I was halfway there when my confidence and security suddenly drained away, as though someone had pulled a plug.

The ground to my right seemed to leap up at me, and the deep black hole to my left felt as though it was sucking me down. I became aware of the heat rising up and rippling over my leg and side. I shook my head as I pictured myself tumbling down, head over heels. I froze, gripping the brickwork as tightly as I had ever held anything. I closed my eyes and tried to wish myself down to the ground and safety.

My stillness was shattered by shouts and angry cries from below. Ted was furious: he thought I was fooling around and delaying him. Anger at his lack of concern, together with fury that he had witnessed my failure, rose within me and sparked me into movement.

I reached around, tore the chains and fittings from their place, and hurled them to the ground. Then, without looking back, I swung a leg backward over the ladder and climbed down to the ground. Ted was waiting at the bottom, hands on his hips and sharp words on his tongue. I ignored him.

"That's it! I've had enough! I'm leaving! Today— now!" I told him, turning and walking away. I didn't care if I never saw another ladder in my life.

I decided that thrills were better if they were had

at other people's expense, so I turned my attention back to the pubs and the closing time fights. I didn't care much that I didn't have a job. In only a couple of months, I would be on my way to Spain for the summer.

As the train jerked to a stop in the Nottingham station, I gathered up the few belongings left from my time in Spain and headed home. In the days to come, it was obvious that that summer had been a turning point in my life. Before, I had always been wild, yet still managed to rein myself in enough to complete a good day's work. But my summer of excess had ruined me for what now seemed a very ordinary, boring life.

To start with, I resented having to pay for my drinks! Having enjoyed a summer of free beer and Bacardi, I hadn't realized how much my consumption had rocketed—nor the demands it would make on my wallet. I quickly found that all my savings were being poured over the counter in the pubs and clubs I frequented.

I was in terrible shape physically. Heavy drinking and poor diet had taken their toll on my body. The wiry condition, built into me by bricklaying, was gone. I was exhausted after just a few hours of bending, straightening, and carrying bricks. I had a hangover until lunch, and getting up for work by 8:00 a.m. seemed like a cruel punishment.

At lunch time, I went to the nearest pub for a few beers to try to keep me going for the rest of the day. More often than not, though, it turned into an afternoon's drinking binge, and I wouldn't make it back to work. My reputation among the foremen was not good, and my many absences meant my pay packet was often slim at the end of the week.

It was an endless spiral. The world seemed to be in conspiracy against me, forcing me ever downward. What I couldn't admit to myself was that in addition to being an alcoholic, I was also a full-blown drug addict. I had consumed such huge quantities of speed and hash during the months in Spain that my body burned without it. I managed to find a few drug contacts in the shabbier pubs of Nottingham, but it was never as readily available as it had been at the Crazy Horse Saloon.

When I wasn't able to get the drugs I desperately needed, I sank into deep, dark depression. I had never been particularly sociable at the best of times, but during these times of depression, I withdrew into myself. The most ordinary attempt to make conversation felt like a physical attack. I avoided talking to people, remaining at the bar drinking alone, or disappeared into my room at home.

Relationships were at an all-time low. My family was visibly shocked over my physical condition, but I would not talk to them about what was happening to me. I simply used home as a shelter: somewhere to lay my head before stumbling out in search of another drink or another blast of dope.

The offer of work in Switzerland was like a lifeline to a drowning man. It had come completely out of the blue, in a letter from a friend from the Crazy Horse Saloon who knew someone opening a new hotel in the fashionable ski resort of Hoyt Nandes, near Sion. He wanted to know if I was interested in working as a waiter there.

The Bluesy Hotel was nothing like the Crazy Horse Saloon. It was well built, tastefully decorated, and a haunt for the wealthy. Soon after arriving, I found myself learning French so that my serving style matched my sharp, new uniform. It was a far cry from what I was used to, but I enjoyed the new environment in a strange way. I threw myself into learning how to inquire after Monsieur's choice of wine, and what dish to recommend to Madame.

In addition to waiting on tables in the small restaurant, I was put in charge of the coffee shop and bar. Such responsibilities suited me. I may have been enjoying the new job, but that didn't stop me from trying to rob my employer at every opportunity. I took a bottle of the best red wine to a customer, collected his money, and then somehow forgot to ring it up on the cash register. Soon I had another small mountain of money piling up in my room.

My plan was to amass as much as I could in as short a time as possible, and then disappear. Before I could pull all the loose ends together, however, a beat-up old camper van pulled into the parking lot one night. Out of it hopped two young American travelers who were passing through.

Harvey and his friend were students, taking some time out from their studies to see Europe. Their money was running low, so they were looking for work to help tide them over. My friend from Spain had found the quietness of the Swiss hotel scene too much and had left. In the wake of his departure, I was given the responsibility of running the disco and the restaurant. Being short-staffed, I hired Harvey and his friend.

The night they arrived, we sat and chatted in my room. As we did, Harvey reached into his travel bag. My words dried on my lips, and my mouth fell open as he pulled out one well-wrapped package after another. It was the biggest haul of hash I had ever seen—enough to keep a dealer in the lap of luxury for years back in England. Just seeing the drug set my juices flowing, and I licked my lips as he peeled the plastic covering off the greenish-brown substance and smiled. "Ever tried this, Johnny?"

Then he broke off a big chunk, crumbled it, and we rolled it into several cigarettes. The rest of the night passed in a delightful haze of warm, cotton-wool feelings as the drug flowed through my bloodstream like a welcome old friend.

The pattern was set. Soon we were smoking hash for breakfast, lunch, and dinner. The days disappeared into a blur of late nights, talking, laughing, and smoking. We raced through the dull days of serving dinners so that we could get to our next hash time. In addition to the physical pleasure it brought, I sensed I was on the edge of something else.

I sat for hours with Harvey and his friend, pungent smoke whirling around us. Our talk invariably turned to the meaning of life. "You see, man," Harvey said, "It's all about finding yourself. You've got to find yourself—where you've come from, where it's all at. You know what I mean?"

"Yeah, Harvey," I nodded. "I think I do. Tell me some more." I was never actually sure what he was talking about, but the earnest way in which he said it convinced me that he must be right. It all sounded so good. There was something, somewhere just beyond me, where I could belong—something I could find and be a part of. The prospect excited me in a way that drinking, fighting, and sleeping around never did. It was a curious sensation of discovery; a sensation which I wanted to last.

But then the mood changed, and we were rolling on the floor, our sides almost bursting with laughter over a silly incident that had occurred during the course of the day. The hash seemed to bring my emotions to the surface in a way I had never experienced. At last I was experiencing feelings other than anger, resentment, jealousy, rage, and aggression. My emotions bubbled over, splashing down around me.

In that blue-gray smoky atmosphere, it was as though a cork had been removed from me, and like champagne, my pent-up emotions burst forth like a rich, rare vintage. After our discussions, I felt as though I had been let in on one of the biggest and best-kept secrets in the universe. There was more to life!

Oftentimes, the hash seemed to excite my taste buds, and I was overcome by a sudden, ravenous hunger. We tiptoed down to the hotel kitchen and sneaked away with a dozen or so chocolate bars. Back in our room, we gorged on the chocolate, reveling in its sticky sweetness.

The following morning, I awoke with a headache and nausea. I was never sure whether it was the chocolate or the drugs that made me feel that way. I preferred to think it was the chocolate; I didn't want to believe that anything that made me feel so wonderfully calm could possibly dump me like that the next morning.

With such a ready supply of hash available, our appetite for it grew out of all proportion. Soon we were stoned almost around the clock. It took every drop of energy to hold my head together on everyday matters, like serving behind the bar and giving people the right change, or the wrong—if I knew there was a chance I could rip them off.

Harvey's friend only worked for a short time at the Bluesy Hotel before moving on in search of more adventure. It turned out that he and Harvey had been trying to peddle their slabs of hash along the way, but with little success. Switzerland didn't take kindly to drugs, hard or soft, so they had not been able to make many inroads. That's why they came looking for work to tide them over financially.

After several weeks, Harvey and I decided to move, as well. We quit our jobs, hung up our work clothes for the last time, and set out together on an overland trek through Europe. With all the money I had earned and stolen during my time at the hotel, we were well provided for, and passed an enjoyable two months staying at youth hostels, eating and drinking well, smoking dope, and all the while, feeling an increasing need to "find ourselves."

We went to Athens, Corfu, and finally on to Crete, where we rented a small apartment and moved in with a couple of girls we had met at a harbor bar. Every day we bought cases of beer. Life was one long party. Finally, though, May arrived, and with it the start of another summer season at the Crazy Horse Saloon. Harvey and I had our last drink together and waved each other a cheery goodbye—each to continue our own search for something we weren't quite sure of.

Back in Spain, it was more of the same from the previous year. All-night partying in the bar, a different girl every night, and late mornings spent trying to recover from the previous night's activities.

Yet somehow, I seemed to be losing my taste for it all. It was like a bottle of soda pop left open too long—all the ingredients were there, but the fizz was gone. I actually found myself, on occasions, dreading the prospect of having to go through the motions of passion with another sunburned, vodka-fueled, pleasure-seeking girl.

Even the fighting spirit in me was ebbing away. It was partly because of my increasingly heavy drug use, which slowed down my emotions, but it also reflected a growing sense that I was somehow missing out on something more meaningful in life. Now and then I tried to talk about it with the other guys at the Crazy Horse Saloon, but they just laughed me off.

"Do you ever wonder what it's all about—life, I mean?" I'd casually ask over a breakfast beer.

"What d'ya mean, Johnny? It's women and drinking, isn't it? What more could you want, eh?"

Someone else chipped in, "Not thinking of becoming a monk, are you, Johnny? Just because you didn't score last night." And my honest question was drowned in a sea of guffaws and giggles.

But I couldn't shake my inner restlessness. I watched the young vacationers come in, dressed in their best evening clothes. They'd drink more than they should, and stagger away in the early hours of the morning, laughing and hooting. It all seemed so empty to me. "Surely there's got to be more to life than working at some dead-end job for fifty weeks of the year so you can come to Spain and be hung over in the sun!" I said to myself.

Finally, I became so unsettled that I had to do something about it. So one day, I quit my job and set out to see if I could find answers to the questions that haunted me.

I found my way to Marrakesh, a hot and dusty city in Morocco. I stayed in a cheap hotel, and began hanging around the bars and hotels where intense young travelers from all over Europe gathered to share their drugs and hunger for reality.

Some days, I consumed more dope than my hash-saturated system could take, and was unable to do anything but lie on my bed, stare up at the cracked ceiling, and listen to the buzz of circling flies. Shouts erupted in the street below and wafted up to my room. I longed for someone to come tell me what was going on as I lay pinned to my bed.

Then depression overcame me. Great, black clouds of gloom overwhelmed me. I felt trapped by the foreboding of some uncertain, but huge, catastrophe. Eating and washing seemed unimportant. I became suspicious of the other travelers, thinking they were out to steal my money or dope. Everywhere I went, I constantly checked behind me, convinced someone was trying to sneak up on me.

Such paranoia finally drove me from Morocco to Gibraltar. By then, my funds were low, so I managed to get a few days' work bricklaying at a new hotel complex. At the same time, I bought two expensive cameras and a cassette tape player on credit, then left Gibraltar within a few days, selling the equipment for cash when I arrived in Spain.

Soon I was back at the Crazy Horse Saloon, anxious to tell everyone about my travels and experiences. I stayed there for a couple of weeks, but the job no longer held any appeal. Moving on to Lorette, I shared an apartment with Fanta, whom I had met at the saloon. He shared my appetite for hash, and we began pushing it in the town, as well as smoking huge quantities ourselves.

When the summer season finally ended, it was time to head back to Nottingham once more. I arrived home, little more than skin and bone, withdrawn and suspicious of everyone around me. There were large, raw ulcers in my mouth, which meant that on the rare occasions when I felt like eating, I couldn't, because it was too painful. My lips were sore and cracked, and I was plagued with stomach cramps.

Somehow, I managed to stumble back to my parents' house, where the full extent of my physical slump hit me. When Mom opened the door, she hardly recognized me; she just cried.

By then, I was beyond holding down a job. I made one or two attempts to resume bricklaying, but the demands of being on time and the physical hardships were too much for me. More often than not, I simply lay in bed until late morning, then shuffled down to the local pub to drink away the afternoon.

I managed to make enough contacts around town to feed my drug craving, but I didn't feel the freedom to smoke it at home. So I moved into a dirty, one-room apartment a couple of streets away. It had a bed with some dirty linens, a shabby old wardrobe, a broken chair, and a sink. As well as making me more docile, the drugs reduced my sex drive. When I did feel the urge and tried to lure a girl away from the crowd, my unkempt, unshaven, and unwashed appearance invariably repulsed her.

Then one morning I bent over the sink in my damp attic apartment and looked into the mirror. Staring back at me was an old, haggard man with sunken eyes, yellowed teeth, and deeply etched lines around his mouth and eyes. As I examined my face, I remembered the time on top of the industrial chimney, balancing, the dark drop in front of me. The similarity of the situations struck me.

"You're falling apart, Johnny," I told myself. "You're on the edge. If you aren't careful, you're going to fall into the flames."

I was worried. The face staring back at me didn't seem to care.

7

The Silent Scream

I was flying off to start a brand new life—so I got drunk to celebrate. Together with a gang of other bricklayers, I boarded a plane at London's Heathrow Airport on my way to Canada and a bright new future.

The realization that I was literally wasting away had hit me hard that day in my shabby apartment. I had not been able to shake the sense of alarm it provoked. It had remained with me as things went from bad to worse.

With every spare penny going to buy drink and drugs, I'd fallen well behind in my rent payments. When I knew the landlord was coming (I could hear the barking of his two fierce dogs well down the street), I turned off the stereo and lights, lying quietly on my bed while waiting for him to stop knocking and go away. I heard him curse and kick the door as he stomped off.

One day, though, he caught me leaving the building and bluntly told me: "I want you out, Goodfellow. You owe me money, and you're nothing but trouble. You've got to get out."

My parents let me move back into my old room. If they were worried about me, they weren't prepared to say anything. But moving back home prompted me to try work again. I soon found myself back on the building sites for a time. During one lunch break, I casually picked up a newspaper that had been tossed aside by one of the other men.

I flipped through the pages idly, until I came to the classified advertisement section. As I scanned down the columns, one ad caught my eye: "Canada. Top rates for bricklayers. Free flights, good money. Apply now for further information." I read on, drinking in the details about the money waiting to be earned in beautiful Canada. It sounded so wonderful, a welcome relief from the cold, wet monotony of the Midlands.

Perhaps this is what I need, I thought. *A new place. New friends. New prospects. A chance to break with the past and build a new future.* I'd been able to discipline myself to work hard in the past. Here was an opportunity to do so once more. I could do it. I could pull myself together, if I really tried. I could save myself from complete collapse. All I needed was determination, effort, and willpower. I carefully tore the ad from the page and slipped it into my pocket.

I called the number listed in the advertisement, and was invited to Birmingham for an interview. After being accepted for the job, I'd simply had to wait for all my paperwork to be processed. Less than ten days later, I was off to Heathrow to join other bricklayers—including two of my Nottingham work mates—for a flight to Canada. Three times the salary of Britain, bracing fresh air, and fine living—we toasted each other's good fortune from take-off to touchdown. The airborne party was a sort of farewell to my old life. I was determined to turn my life around in the days ahead.

And I did. We had been contracted to work on a major new apartment complex in St. John, New Brunswick, on Canada's eastern seaboard. Local laborers didn't like working during the harsh winters, and managed to make enough money during the summer months so they didn't have to. Hence the need to recruit British bricklayers to keep the project moving through the winter.

For the first week, we were housed at a comfortable hotel in town, after which time we were expected to find our own accommodations. I rented a smart studio apartment not far from the building site. It was clean, cozy, and convenient, and I soon felt as though I'd found myself a new home.

The work was hard, but with my determination to make a new start, I responded willingly. On some mornings, it was so cold that big fan heaters had to be set blowing on each level of the building to keep the freshly-mixed mortar from freezing and cracking before we could use it. There were days when the temperature was twenty-five degrees below freezing. But though it was colder than Nottingham, it was also cleaner, and I enjoyed breathing the crisp morning air.

I had resolved from the beginning to keep my head down and work hard. I wanted to make as much money as quickly as possible. I was looking for a home, a wife, and a family—and I figured that by pulling myself together and really trying, I could make it all happen for me. So I disciplined myself hard. No drugs, no crazy nights, no heavy drinking.

At the end of the day I was tired; my body was still getting used to the hard labor. I returned to my room, weary but satisfied, washed and changed, and headed down the street to a nearby bar.

There I enjoyed a leisurely meal of steak and plenty of vegetables, followed by no more than four or five quiet beers with a few of the other regular patrons. (This amount was but a sip when compared to my former intake of alcohol). Then I strolled back to my room and climbed into bed for a contented night's sleep, satisfied with my work, and looking forward to the prospects of the next day.

This pattern continued for several weeks, until one Friday night. As I headed along the corridor to my apartment, I accidentally collided with someone walking in the opposite direction. He was a tall, broad, bearded French-Canadian named Frankie, who had just moved in. As we stepped away from each other, we looked up, and I mumbled an apology.

He looked at me for a moment and then asked matter-of-factly: "Do you smoke dope?"

"Sure I do," I answered quickly and eagerly, as a part of me seemed to stand back and look in horror as all my resolutions and plans were swept away in an instant. Even as we turned and headed back to his room, I was appalled at the way in which all my efforts seemed to be crumbling to nothing. But my feelings were swamped by an overwhelming desire to feel the wonderful rush of floating freedom that came with smoking a joint. I only hoped it was good hash.

It was, and my period of abstinence seemed to add to the anticipation. Frankie and I sat down and swapped hash stories as he took the hash from his hiding place, burned it over some silver paper, and then rolled it into two large joints. The familiar, pungent, smoky sweetness made my nose wrinkle as I drew heavily on my joint.

We spent several hours getting thoroughly stoned before going out on the town. In a series of bars and discos, I managed to spend most of the money I'd earned during my brief time in Canada. We returned to our rooms with empty pockets, but each with a woman on our arm. They stayed the night, and we alternately slept and smoked until dawn. Though it was Saturday, I was due on the job, as I worked six or seven days each week.

I decided not to go. Instead, the four of us stayed in our rooms, smoking and drinking the weekend away. I awoke on Tuesday morning, feeling hung over, heavy-headed, and defeated. All the pleasure of the weekend drained away as I realized that my best efforts had come to nothing. I was back where I had started, and there didn't seem to be anything I could do about it.

An ongoing struggle began. I tried to make sure I arrived in time for work every morning, while at the same time trying to enjoy wild night life again. Some nights, Frankie and I were out dancing and drinking until 3:00 a.m., returning for a couple of hours of fitful sleep before arising at 6:30.

Soon I was turning up on the job only two or three mornings a week—putting in just enough hours to cover the costs of my accommodation, drink, and drugs. My erratic work schedule slimmed my pay packet so much that I finally had to move from my comfortable lodgings to less tasteful accommodation in a poorer part of town.

I couldn't bring myself to tell my family back home what was happening to me. My first letters, after arrival, had been enthusiastic and cheerful. I told them how exciting Canada was, and how well things were going for me. As I slipped back into my old ways, I began to make my notes briefer and less frequent, until eventually I stopped writing at all. Except for one short note—to tell them I was getting married.

I met Corinne in a disco one night, and was attracted to her immediately. She was a beautiful French-Canadian woman with an oval face, dark, brown eyes, and long, dark hair. I started talking to her over a drink, and so began a relationship that blossomed in the days that followed.

Although fairly quiet by nature, she enjoyed the excitement of nightlife, too, and after an evening's drinking in the bars and clubs, we headed back to my apartment with a bottle of whiskey and some hash. Within a few weeks, I asked her to marry me, and she accepted. We intended to get married in a matter of months, so we moved in together.

Corinne made me happy, and lessened the disappointment I was feeling over my failure to make a clean break. Here was someone who shared my love for the buzz of drugs and alcohol, but was able to help me keep it all under some sort of control. Perhaps it was possible to tread a middle line, after all.

I told myself that Corinne made me feel different than all the other girls had made me feel. There had been plenty of other women, but they had been objects to me, not people. I had never felt comfortable talking to them, never thought of them as people with needs, feelings, and hurts. I was only interested in whether or not they'd go to bed with me, and how to drop them afterward without a scene.

It was partly a horrible sense of awkwardness and partly deep insecurity that kept me from getting close emotionally to a woman. I never got used to that awful moment when you had to go up and ask a girl if she wanted to dance. I dreaded her saying "no," and the feelings of rejection and ridicule I experienced in front of my friends. So I kept women at arm's length, except in bed. I was baffled by the way I desperately wanted to pursue women, but didn't seem able to get close once I'd caught one. The threat of true intimacy frightened me.

It had seemed otherwise for a time with Sharon. At eighteen, I had met her in a Nottingham club, a slim, blonde secretary from a respectable, middle-class home. It was before my life had begun its slide into the wild side, and we began a courtship that seemed stable and contented. One day, she looked ashen as we met after work, and blurted out: "Johnny, you'll never believe it: I'm pregnant!"

The shock threw us together. We were terrified about what our parents would say, but there seemed to be no way out. We faced two sets of silent, saddened parents as we told them what had happened, and began to plan for the future. Initially, we intended to get married, but as the plans became more serious, I started to panic.

With little thought for Sharon and the child she carried, all I could see was my freedom being taken away from me. I was a young man with a future ahead of me. I was too young to be stuck at home with a wife, a child, and responsibilities. The prospect alarmed me. So, in an emotional scene, I told Sharon it was all off, then turned and walked out of her life to concentrate on my own.

Memories of that failed relationship flooded back as Corinne and I discovered that ours would not be a smooth path to the altar. At first, being with her had curbed my excessive appetite for drugs, but her presence gradually began to act less and less as a brake. I got heavily stoned, or drank myself to a standstill, and we argued about it. The way I pushed myself to the limits frightened her, despite her own love of getting high.

Things came to a head one night in my room, and Corinne walked out on me. I collapsed on the bed after she left, and stared up at the bare electric bulb swinging from the ceiling. I listened as her footsteps faded down the corridor. I knew I would never see her again. The cottage with the roses around the door and the smiling kids would never be.

I didn't know what to feel. It was as though I were awake under an anesthetic—conscious of my body and the reality of what had just happened to me, but beyond feeling anything. My last flicker of hope about starting a new life had been snuffed out, and I was beyond reacting.

Water dripped maddeningly into the cracked, rust-stained wash basin in the corner of the room. Cold air drifted up through the cracks in the bare, wooden floorboards, chilling my ankles. But I did not flinch. I just stared up at the ceiling and ran my tongue, thick with alcohol, over my dry lips. Then a thought crossed my mind. It was definite and direct.

I had totally lost control of my life.

At first it was just a fact, unavoidable and unarguable. But then it became a gate that slowly began to open, allowing a flood of emotion to come crashing through. A wave of cold, sharp fear surged through me as I tried to look into the future, and realized there was absolutely nothing to see. There wasn't even the faintest straw to which I could cling. I was drowning in the sea of my own failure.

Each new realization beat upon me like waves against a cliff. No one knew I was lying in a filthy room alone. No one cared. I had no friends I could call for help. My drinking was out of control. I couldn't get enough drugs to satisfy my craving. And it was beyond me to show any care or concern for another human being. Tomorrow was just a black hole.

My life passed before me in a series of explosive, empty episodes that appalled, overwhelmed, and terrified me. I couldn't move. All I could do was lie on top of my broken-down old brass bed and stare at the ceiling.

Suddenly, I jerked forward in an agonizing wrench as a scream burst from my lips. But there was no sound. My mouth was open wide and my teeth were bared, but it was a silent scream—an inward shriek at the horror confronting me. It was like vomiting despair.

Falling backward onto the bed, I drifted into a welcome, alcoholic sleep, half hoping I wouldn't wake up in the morning. I didn't want to live through another pointless, hopeless day.

But I awoke the next morning, cold, cramped, and hung over. I knew something strange and frightening had happened to me. It had been more than just the effects of drugs and alcohol. Something had been clawing at my heart. I knew I had to get as far away from the situation as I could. I had to leave Canada at once.

My final reason for staying in Canada had fallen through, together with my hopes for a new start in life. With Corinne out of my life, there was no way that I could stay, whether I wanted to or not. Two months earlier, there had been an early morning visit to the building site by some officials from the Canadian government.

They turned out to be men from the Immigration Department, and their investigations had revealed that a number of British bricklayers—including me—had made false declarations to get the necessary papers that would allow us into Canada. I had failed to admit to my criminal record from the jewelry store break-in. The officials had found out about it, and wanted me out of the country.

Only my engagement to Corinne had rescued me from certain deportation. Anyone marrying a Canadian citizen automatically won the relevant authorization to stay in the country. With our engagement over, my papers would soon find their way to the top of the immigration department's "action" tray.

The morning after Corinne's departure, I knew I had to leave. I was emotionally and physically beaten, like a whipped dog. I just wanted to crawl into a quiet place and wait for it all to be over. With the little money I had saved, I bought an airline ticket, and the next day, boarded a plane for home.

As I stepped off the plane at Heathrow, my mind dared look no further than getting through customs. If there was any point or hope in life, it was beyond my grasp. I shuffled into the line at the exit that seemed to echo my despair: "Nothing to declare."

8

Beyond Reality

No one ever asked what had happened to my plans for a bright new life. They didn't have to; one look at me told the whole story of failure. I was thin and sickly, and any shred of confidence I ever possessed had been stripped away by my experiences in Canada. I was cowed and quiet, and tried to avoid talking with people in any situation. I just couldn't cope with trying to communicate.

Being at home again was dreadful. To relieve the agony and boredom, I headed to the pub, where I bought a beer and sat, withdrawn, in a corner or up against the bar. I sipped my beer and watched the people around me laugh and joke. I felt isolated from it all, as though viewing it through a one-way mirror. I could see them, but I could not interact at all.

Life had become a mechanical round of dragging myself out of bed, shuffling through the day until the bars opened, drinking silently until they closed, then falling into bed for a restless night's sleep. The whole meaningless cycle repeated itself the next day.

Then one night, I was at the Flying Horse, sitting in the corner slowly sipping my beer and watching

the chatter and drinking around me. I spotted someone I thought I recognized from long ago. We got to
talking as he waited to be served, and he turned out
to be an old school friend, Alan. But he had changed.

Back at school, I had been recognized as one of
the leaders—because of my temper and talent for
fighting. But Alan, tall, thin, and quiet, had just been
another one of the boys. This time, though, I was
introspective and unsure of myself and everyone
else, while Alan seemed to be just the opposite.

Dressed in a smart leather jacket, Alan bought me
a beer as a gesture of casual generosity, then men-
tioned that his sports car was parked outside. I got
the impression that he was doing really well for
himself, although he was rather vague about what
he actually did for a living. Whatever it was, it certainly seemed lucrative.

Alan and I struck up a friendship as we recalled
our school days and some of the people we had
known. By the end of the evening, we had agreed to
meet again the following night to score some dope.

Over the next few weeks, Alan and I became close
friends. We drank together until closing time, then
went back to his apartment across town. There we
smoked hash until we nodded off to sleep in the
small hours of the morning.

I soon discovered that Alan's successful appearance was only that. He was out of work and was
already several month's payments behind on his
sports car. I sensed that, in his own way, Alan was
just as empty inside as I was.

One evening, as we sat drowsily in his flat, drawing on a joint and talking, Alan asked me unexpectedly: "Do you ever think about spiritual things,
Johnny?"

I squinted at him through the smoke, furrowing my eyebrows. "Eh? Spiritual things? What do you mean?"

"Well, you know. Life. Don't you ever wonder what life's about, like—why we are here and all? You know, the future, death, and all that?"

My heart started to race, but somehow I didn't dare confess my curiosity about those things. I was too frightened to open up and expose what was really inside—the horrible feelings of emptiness, loneliness, and uncertainty.

I responded in a non-committal way: "No, I can't say I've thought about that stuff in years." But not wanting him to stop talking, I added, "Why do you ask that, Alan?"

He got up quickly and walked over to a wall cupboard. Rummaging about in it, he pulled out a large, black book. He sat next to me on the sofa, and dropped the book onto the coffee table in front of us.

"Well, I was wondering if you were interested in any of this," he said, pointing at the book. The cover proclaimed in large gold letters, *Hidden and Forbidden Knowledge.*

I picked up the book and flipped through it. I sensed that Alan was trying to share his excitement with me. Flipping through the pages of the thick volume, I saw photographs and articles about tarot cards, astrology, astral projection, clairvoyance, and black magic. There were even guidelines for magic rites and drawing pentagrams and other symbols.

The pages seemed to leap out at me. This was what I had been looking for! There really were answers to the questions I had been asking myself. I pored over the pages, thrilled by this whole new world that was opening before me, full of meaning and purpose.

When I finally left Alan's apartment that night, I had *Hidden and Forbidden Knowledge* tucked under my arm.

For the next two weeks, I spent almost every waking moment studying the book with a strange compulsion. I couldn't understand all that it said, but I saw enough to know that this was extremely important. My whole life was in the balance, and here was the answer.

From then on, Alan and I talked about nothing else. We read sections of the book together, discussed what various aspects meant, and how they might be applied to our lives. We became particularly drawn to astrology and the idea that our lives might in some way be influenced by the alignment of the planets and the stars.

This possibility both attracted and repelled me. I was filled with hope by the idea that all those times that I had spun out of control—violence, drugs, and sex—may have been beyond my governing. But I was also consumed by dread with the prospect that what happened in the heavens was charting my future. There may be worse things still ahead for me.

Every day, I read what the newspaper astrologers had to say for Aquarius, but I soon began to dismiss their columns as trivial. Through visiting occult book shops and buying more literature, Alan and I began to realize that there was a far deeper side to this whole new world than most people realized.

Soon, Alan's pretty blonde girlfriend, Sarah, and her roommate, Jenny, joined us, and the four of us spent long evenings discussing the things we were reading about. Alan and I tried to make objects move by psychokinesis, and there were occasions when I really believed that the mug on the table in front of me was shimmering and vibrating because of the power we were releasing from within.

We also became fascinated by what we read about astral projection. These were mystical out-of-body experiences that people apparently had after going into a trance. Their inner being, or spirit, was freed from their physical body, and they were able to travel to different places and dimensions, and learn new and secret truths about life. Despite fueling our efforts to fall into a trance with larger and larger quantities of drugs, Alan and I were frustrated by our failure to travel on these incredible out-of-body journeys.

Sarah and Jenny were more successful, though—and it frightened them. One evening, Sarah told us how the night before, she had found herself leaving her body as she was drawn into the astral plane. Suddenly, she was looking in the bathroom mirror—but a different face stared back. She turned to look back into the bedroom...and saw her own body lying in bed. The experience shocked her deeply, and she never tried to "travel" like that again.

Alan and I were excited by her account, though, and it only added to our sense of annoyance that we had not managed to achieve similar things. We felt we were very close to something; quite what, we didn't really know, but it was a matter of life or death to us.

We felt as though we had been let in on a secret that was too big for the rest of the world. We were on the edge of something so important that only a few people could be trusted with it.

Houses, cars, and children playing in the park were what most people thought of as "real." But if they only knew what we knew! In a crazy way, everything around us was unreal, but a greater reality lay just a hair's breadth away. It was so tantalizingly close, but just out of reach. There were keys to understanding and power that unlocked the universe. They were such important keys that they were not made known to ordinary people—only to those who hungered for deeper reality.

Alan and I felt we were part of a select group who had been chosen for the revelation of those keys. Some of the others had formed rock groups and had hidden secret messages in the music they weaved. To us, Hawkwind, Pink Floyd, and Jethro Tull were musical prophets, speaking of deep things. We spent hours searching every phrase and tone of their songs, looking for coded words and information.

Our search became so obsessive that we spoke about nothing else. But while we felt we'd been especially chosen to learn about the hidden landscapes of life, we also felt a responsibility to share some of what we were learning with others.

We tried to explain to our drinking partners in the pubs and clubs how the world was on the brink of a series of cataclysmic events, and that people had to find the keys to unlock the past, present, and future. Neither the blank stares of incomprehension, nor the nickname "The Prophets of Doom," which we quickly earned, put us off. We knew, deep inside, that our quest was too important to be derailed by people's lack of understanding.

Alan suggested that one way we could be helped in our search would be to seek guidance from the country's top astrologer. We had read all his best-selling books on the subject. Perhaps if we showed him our commitment to finding the truth, he would be able to help. After hearing of his weekly meetings in London to discuss astrological issues, we excitedly traveled down one Wednesday to take part.

It was a crushing disappointment. We had been expecting to find a man of hypnotic attraction—a leader. Instead, he was a rather nondescript, quiet little man who couldn't even look us in the eyes when we introduced ourselves. The other members of the group—whom we had anticipated would be like an inner circle of devotees—seemed no more than a group of middle-aged, middle-class suburbanites with a passing fancy for astrology.

We stayed for the meeting, and listened to an elderly man with big, bushy eyebrows babble on about some obscure aspect of astrology. We left in despair. Our high hopes had been dashed. We felt cheated, yet at the same time, agreed that while they had only been playing at it, our exploration of the meaning of life was deadly serious.

In some ways, this disappointment only sharpened our desire to find the truth, and we spent more and more time locked in study, trying to fall into trances, and searching acid rock music for messages and guidance.

Our search consumed our nights and days. We sat up into the early hours of the morning, when a restless kind of sleep finally overtook us. By then, I was working as a self-employed bricklayer, so if I didn't feel like going to work the next morning, I didn't go. The money I earned as a sub-contractor, when I did work, made up for the days I missed.

The days I stayed at home, Alan and I met over lunch to talk about our thoughts and studies. Then we went to the pub and drank and talked until afternoon closing time. From there, we headed back either to Alan's or my place. (I had once again moved away from home, much to my family's combined relief and concern, and found a shabby room to rent

in the building where Sarah and Jenny lived.) There
we smoked some dope, which kept us going until
evening, when there was another round of drinking,
drugs, and talk about "the keys."

I was joined in my erratic work arrangements by
a group of other self-employed bricklayers, one of
whom was Mac. Big, broad, and sharp-featured, Mac
loved to drink and womanize, and was always in the
thick of the fun. (I had known him from my times in
Spain and Canada.) Yet when Mac heard about the
search Alan and I were on, he didn't just laugh it off
and disappear for another drink. He began asking
questions about what we were doing, and gradually
joined our nightly sessions of study, drink, and
dope. With him came Gary, whom we also knew
from the local drinking scene.

Shorter than Mac, with a mass of thick, curly
black hair, Gary had been married, but was separated from his wife. He always seemed to have
plenty of money, but no one was ever quite sure
where it all came from. And it was best not to ask.

Among the four of us, we had sampled just about
everything life had to offer. Yet as we sat together,
drinking, talking, and smoking, we all agreed that
for all the action we had experienced, there was still
an emptiness inside. While we were only in our early
and mid-twenties, in some ways we felt like old men
with nothing to look forward to. Only the prospect
of there being something else, something outside
ourselves, held any hope.

One night, as we were all squeezed into my dirty
room, finishing off a couple of joints, I suddenly felt
as though the clouds in my head parted, and I could
see the way ahead clearly.

"You know, guys, we've got to find God."

They just looked at me and waited for me to continue.

"Look, we all know that there's more to life than what people see out there, right?" I asked as I pointed to the street below. "Well, then, there must be some kind of supreme power or being who's in control of the universe, right? And if we can find him, then he—or it, or whatever—will be able to help us understand ourselves; show us all the mysteries we're searching for."

Alan agreed: "Yeah...that's right, Johnny. We all believe that there is some supreme being out there. So it must be able to be found—and when we do find it, we'll find the answers."

We all started to grin and nod to each other. There was a thrill of excitement as we felt we had really hit on something important. We crammed into Alan's car and drove into town, where we went to Frodo's, a noisy cellar wine bar, to celebrate.

We got truly drunk that night, and when people asked what our toasts were about, we grinned and told them: "We're going to find God!"

The sense of euphoria carried us over the next few days, and we began to discuss how we might start to search for God. We agreed that we should begin by seeking help from holy men who might be able to put us on the right track.

The church never entered our thinking. We had all had similar experiences with a sterile faith that mouthed love and mocked sincerity, and we dismissed Christianity as being as empty as the collection plates that we had all passed along the pew in our younger days.

Until this point, the people in our drinking circles had humored our talk about the supernatural world, but with the pub-time planning sessions for our search to find God, some people began to get more concerned.

"Don't you think you're all taking this a bit too far, lads?" they asked from time to time. A few even dared to catch one of the others when they were alone and cautiously suggest that perhaps I really needed to see a doctor.

One day, I read about a band of mystics who lived in the remote mountains of Iran. They were deeply spiritual nomads who performed ancient rites in their communion with the gods. As I read, I knew that I had found the route we needed to follow.

I filled the others in about these horse-riding gurus, and said: "These are the men. These are the ones who can help us find God. We've got to go and find them."

It became clear, as we pooled our limited assets, that we didn't have the money needed to fund such a trip. My fear of the future spurred me to action. I had to explore this hazy world of spiritual things, yet I was frightened to do so alone. By encouraging the others, I could persuade them to join me.

With the desperate passion for meaning driving me, I took on the role of ringleader, and began to scheme ways to get us on the road to the Middle East. After a few late nights, I had it, and I called the others together to lay the plan before them.

I told them we needed some initial money. To get it, all we had to do was pull off a fraud. I had done a couple of frauds in the past, and knew it was a quick and easy way to get money. Once we had the amount we needed, we would buy a van and travel overland to Iran. If our money ran short along the way, it would be easy enough for the four of us to find a victim of some sort to provide more.

Alan, Mac, and Gary nodded in agreement. "Sounds good, Johnny. But where do we do all this?"

I didn't hesitate in replying, although I wasn't sure what was going to tumble from my lips as I opened my mouth to speak.

"Amsterdam. We're going to go to Amsterdam, and we'll start from there."

As I said it, I knew that it was right—but I didn't know why. I'd only been to Amsterdam once before, and it had been an experience I was glad to leave behind as quickly as possible.

It had been during my weeks traveling in search of "the scene" to which Harvey had introduced me. I'd heard so much about Amsterdam. It was the fountainhead of the drug trail that wound its way from Europe through the Middle East and beyond.

All kinds of drugs were sold openly on the streets. Some cafes even had little marijuana leaf signs on the windows, and you were able to buy a couple of sticks over the counter, or baked into a cake. "You just have to go to Amsterdam and experience it," I was told. "It's so free and easy, so laid back, so beautiful."

When I arrived at the city's Central Station, my pockets were still bulging from the proceeds of my time at the Crazy Horse Saloon. Yet a crippling sense of fear gripped me almost as soon as I stepped out of the cavernous railway station. There were smiling, dope-hazed faces all around me; young jean-clad groups clustered around guitars on street corners; and graffiti urging "love, not war" everywhere. But I felt completely ill at ease.

I took a quick walking tour of the city, then headed into one of the large parks in the center of the city. Although I had enough money to rent a suite at any of Amsterdam's plushest hotels, I was too scared to set foot inside any of them. So I spent a nervous night sleeping curled up on a park bench, and took the first train out of town in the morning.

Memories of that unsettling visit came back to me. But for some reason, I knew that Amsterdam was the place where we should start our search for God.

There was an awkward kind of farewell at home when I explained to my family that we were "going off traveling for a while." I'd told them a little about my fascination with supernatural things, but they had shown no interest, and I didn't want to try and explain it all then. As I turned to leave, Trish said to Mom in a matter-of-fact voice: "I don't think I'm going to see Johnny again."

In a curious way, she was right.

As Alan, Mac, Gary, and I met at the East Midlands Airport and boarded the plane, we were charged up at the thought of starting our pilgrimage.

"Amsterdam, here we come," I thought, as we were sucked back into our seats by the take-off thrust. I didn't realize what a crossroads it would turn out to be.

9

Caught at the Crossroads

The bus from Schiphol Airport let us off at Central Station in the heart of Amsterdam. Unsure of where to stay, we made some inquiries. "The Shelter—cleanest and cheapest place in the city to stay," was the resounding consensus from the people we asked. Gathering up our bags, we set out for The Shelter, following the directions we had been given.

We wound our way through the center of Amsterdam, over arched bridges that crossed tree-lined canals, and through narrow, dank alleys. Crowds of young people milled around in the city. They seemed happy and carefree, yet I couldn't help but notice those who hung back at the rear of the crowds. Their dark, empty, gray-ringed eyes, emaciated bodies, and tattered clothing announced their slavish addiction to heroin. Like human flotsam, they aimlessly waited for their next fix.

Even in my most desperate days, I had never touched heroin. I had seen its ravages in the lives of those who had tried it, and it terrified me.

Passing these wasted lives crouching in doorways or lying on the street, I heard a warning bell sound within. "You could end up this way if your pilgrimage doesn't work out." I tightened my grip on my bag, increased my pace, and urged the other three to get a move on. I wanted to get away from the source of this terrible thought.

From the crowded square, we pushed through a narrow alley and into the heart of Amsterdam's famed red light district. The heroin addicts and pushers were behind us now—we had entered a new world. Prostitutes sitting in small, red-lit windows, wearing little or nothing, urged us to step inside, draw the curtains, hand over our money, and have some "fun" with them.

As we made our way along, it seemed to me that anything and everything went in this part of Amsterdam. Whatever your sexual inclination, there seemed to be a club to pander to and indulge you.

In days gone by, such a broad-minded, bold liberation would have been heady stuff for me. Like a child let loose in a candy store, I would have been out to sample as much as I possibly could. But now, my consuming passion was finding God! I did little more than cast a faintly-curious eye over all that was going on around me as we traipsed along. By now, our arms were beginning to ache from the weight of our bags.

We finally found the three-story building, tucked away in a side street of one of the rougher quarters of Amsterdam's city center. A small, painted sign at the side of the door announced that it was a "Christian Youth Hostel." The crisp, well-run friendliness that greeted us as we stepped through the door of The Shelter both attracted and repelled us. The place seemed a cross between an army barracks and a hospital. There was an air of cleanliness, orderliness, and drilled routine.

After registering, we were shown to a large dormitory on the first floor. The room was filled with two rows of bunks, enough to accommodate forty people. We picked our way through the rows, testing the mattresses until we had each claimed a sleeping perch. At the end of the room were large lockers, and we transferred our belongings into them.

The Shelter had a stark, Dutch feel about it, with its bare wooden floors and green-tiled walls. Despite the many other young travelers like us in residence, there was an almost unnatural, subdued atmosphere. It called to mind a library rather than a hostel.

The next morning, Alan, Mac, and Gary listened attentively to my plan, the swirling steam from hot coffee wafting up among us as we huddled together around a small table in the dining hall of The Shelter. "It was easy; I traveled down to London by train. When I got to Euston Station, I began making quite a commotion about my lost—nonexistent—luggage. You should've seen the way some of the people looked at me." I took a long draw on my cigarette.

"After my act," I continued, "I reported the 'crime' to the Metropolitan Police and headed back to Nottingham, where I made a claim to the insurance company for my lost luggage. (Of course, before leaving Nottingham, I had arranged for more than adequate travel insurance.) They handed me a check for a good amount. All in all, it was a very profitable day's outing," I added smirkingly.

I sipped some coffee before continuing. "So simple and straightforward. And that's the secret, you know? Simplicity. The art of any good fraud is keeping it simple and uncluttered; the less fanciful the tale you spin, the less likely people are to quiz you about it."

I could see the lights come on in the eyes of the other three. Now they realized why I had them take out travel insurance before leaving Nottingham: we were going to pull off a repeat of my earlier fraud.

In low voices, casting a watchful eye out for eavesdroppers, we made our plans. They were simple, really. From Amsterdam, Alan would go to Belgium, Gary to Germany, and Mac to France, where they would report luggage thefts before returning to Amsterdam. It was then just a matter of claiming the money from our insurance companies, and we would be on our way to the East to find God.

Restlessness, plus a desire to show the others how easy it was, spurred me into going first. So, straight after breakfast, our planning complete, I launched into my part of the plan.

I retraced my steps through the narrow streets of Amsterdam to the Central Station. The station was crowded with young people sitting, lying, talking, and smoking in groups. Rock music blared from radios and guitars, and the smell of marijuana was easily detectable in the cool January air.

I pressed through the crowds into the station. I followed along the parade of shops that runs under the central walkway linking the platforms, until I found a vacant photo booth. I pulled the black curtain closed and fed in the necessary coins.

Moments later, my pictures complete, I pulled back the curtain and stumbled out, rubbing my eyes. I threw up my hands in horror. "My bags, my bags, they're gone. Someone's stolen my bags!" I shouted.

I frantically looked from side to side, then began running through the crowded station, looking everywhere for my nonexistent bags. It was quite a show. Travelers stopped and stared at me as I ran by, crying aloud: "Help, please. Someone's stolen my things!"

I spotted a policeman and ran over to him. "My bags; they're gone! I put them outside the photo booth while I had my pictures taken, and they're gone!" I exclaimed.

The policeman shrugged his shoulders with an air of futility. "What do you expect in Amsterdam?" he inquired in his thick Dutch accent. He'd accepted my story at face value; I was overjoyed. The officer directed me to the nearest police station, where again I poured out my story of stolen bags, being careful to give the illusion of someone distracted and distressed by the loss of their worldly possessions.

With the "crime" duly reported and logged, I headed back to the Central Station, where I made a call to the insurance office in Nottingham. Being careful to inject a note of panic into my voice, I explained to them how my trip to Spain had been ruined by this terrible theft in Amsterdam.

I expected them to tell me that a check would be sent over straight away—that's how it had worked in England. But instead, they told me that they had an overseas office in Amsterdam, and that I should go and lodge my claim there.

As I hung up the phone, my resolve seemed to waver for a moment. Did they know something? Had they brushed me off? I wasn't sure, but the compulsion to get the money and begin our spiritual search drove me in the direction of the address I had been given over the phone.

The office was located in a fashionable old Dutch town house along one of the attractive tourist stretches of canal. It was very plush, and I felt strangely at odds as I stepped inside the office.

My discomfort was heightened when, after brazenly running through my story for the fourth time, the inquiries clerk said: "Just wait a few minutes, would you, please?" I sat in the reception area while the clerk disappeared into a back office. Had he seen through my lies? Could he be calling the police? What do I do now? I could feel my pulse begin to quicken, and the room suddenly felt very stuffy.

Moments later, the clerk returned with another man, and I was greatly relieved when I saw he wasn't wearing a uniform. But my relief turned to alarm as he introduced himself as a claims investigator. It hadn't been like this in England; it had all been so quick and simple that time. Still, there was nothing I could do except recount my story to the claims investigator.

Slowly and methodically, my brain whirring to make sure I didn't alter the facts and trip myself up, I went through it all again. For over an hour, the claims investigator asked me question after question, while I tried to remain as calm and innocent-looking as I could.

Finally, he telephoned my mother to verify my story. She really didn't know enough about what I was doing other than to confirm what I had already told the claims investigator. I could have kissed her!

"Yes, my son is traveling on the Continent, and has some friends in Spain that he might be going to see." The claims investigator put the phone down, and turned to me with a smile.

"Well, Mr. Goodfellow, I'm sorry to have kept you so long. Everything seems in order."

A check was made out. "The amount of this check is for two-thirds of the claim, a check to cover the final one-third of the claim will be sent to you from England shortly," said the claims investigator, as he handed me the check. "You can't be too careful these days, you know," he added by way of apology.

I waved my hand in acceptance of his remarks. "It's okay. I quite understand—you've got to be sure about these things," I said before leaving the office.

Once outside I had to resist the impulse to hold the check to my lips and kiss it. Instead, I tucked it into the inside pocket of my jacket and headed back to The Shelter to report the successful completion of the first stage of our four-part swindle.

Encouraged by my successful fraud, Alan, Gary, and Mac spent the next day taking trains to their pre-arranged foreign cities, pantomiming thefts, reporting them to the local authorities and then returning to Amsterdam.

A great sense of unease about being in Amsterdam gripped me, and I spent a restless, impatient day waiting for the others to return. I had a deep foreboding that something dreadfully important, or importantly dreadful, was about to happen.

My frustration and impatience increased when it became apparent that we wouldn't be able to complete the other three frauds as swiftly as mine. The other insurance companies didn't have overseas offices in Amsterdam, and the Nottingham branches were unhappy about sending out checks for such large amounts of money without first completing some detailed paperwork. It would be at least a week, they said, before payments would be mailed to Amsterdam.

We resigned ourselves to this temporary setback in our schedule, and spent the long hours walking the narrow streets, drinking beer in small, dark bars and scoring dope from some of the young travelers we met. But passing the time this way was proving expensive; the money I made from my insurance swindle was being wastefully frittered away.

"Free Music at The Ark!" I hadn't noticed the small flyer pinned to the wall behind the reception area of The Shelter before. Anything that was free sounded good to us at that point, so we decided to go and investigate.

The icy black water of the River Ij, which cuts through Amsterdam on its way to the North Sea, slapped against the piers at the rear of the Central Station. It even sounded cold. I pulled my coat tight around my neck against the chill of the night as we made our way along the piers.

At the end of a line of house boats, moored at the pier furthest from the station, we found The Ark. The Ark consisted of two old houseboats lashed together. They sat low on the water, and looked rather uninviting. As we drew closer, though, the warm, welcoming sound of pulsing rock beats drifted toward us on the gentle, but biting, breeze.

A young man with shoulder-length white hair, a snowy beard, and a huge grin seemed to be standing guard over the door to The Ark. I reached for my pocket and made gestures about paying for entrance. His grin just grew more broad as he waved us in. "It's okay; it's free. Welcome to The Ark!"

We ducked our heads as we climbed down the steep steps, through the doorway, and into the main room of the boat. The room was long and narrow, and from its far reaches, a rock band pounded out contemporary rhythms. On the floor, bunched around low-level tables scattered across the room, were seated about forty young people like ourselves.

I gazed around the room, taking everything in. As I did so, I became aware that something was missing from this near-normal scene. Like with a "spot the difference" puzzle, I quizzed myself, trying to see what it was. Then it hit me; there wasn't a single beer bottle to be seen. Not only that, but there were only a few spirals of smoke, and none that made your nose wrinkle the way smoke from marijuana does. What I saw confused me; everything looked normal, but it wasn't.

I led the way across the room. Halfway across, a young woman, no more than five feet four inches tall, with long, blonde hair and a fresh, open face, complete with a smile as big as that of the guy at the door, approached us.

"Hi, welcome to The Ark," she greeted us. As she spoke, I found my gaze unwillingly dropping to the floor. It was her eyes—they unnerved me. Big and blue, they seemed to bore right through me, right into my heart, almost as though she could see everything I'd ever done.

Compared to me, she was small and vulnerable, yet I was the one who felt intimidated and unnerved by the encounter. An awkward silence ensued for a few moments, a silence that brought back all my old feelings of insecurity and fear.

Finally she continued, "I'm Sherry. I live here on the boats. There's people who live here from more than ten different nations. We're a Christian community...." I heard her words, but they seemed to roll right by me; I wasn't registering what she was saying.

"Yeah, that's great," I ventured, "Uh, where's the beer?"

"Oh, we're not into that kind of thing," she casually returned. "We don't need to get drunk any more."

"Oh, what about pills, then? What do you take?" I inquired, a glimmer of hope in my voice.

Sherry smiled gently. "No, you don't understand. We're Christians, you see...." She began to explain to me how she and her friends now belonged to Jesus.

Her words seem a million miles away from me; I wasn't hearing them. Instead, a terrifying and over-whelming sense of suffocation had overtaken me; I had to get out of the place—and quickly.

I could almost feel thick, strong fingers closing around my throat. There was something weird and off-center about The Ark, and this strange, peaceful-yet-powerful young lady, whose eyes could bore right through me; I had to get out.

I turned to Alan, Gary, and Mac, who were hov-ering behind me. Thankfully, they didn't seem to have picked up on how unnerved I was.

"No dope, guys, no beer, either. There's nothing here for us; let's go somewhere else." We walked away, leaving Sherry standing in the middle of the room.

Crammed with people stoned out of their heads, thick with smoke, and awash with beer and pills, all pulsing to the sound of loud acid rock; the Para-diso—renowned throughout Europe—was the ref-uge to which we fled after our experience on The Ark. Propped around a table, we steadily worked our way toward oblivion. I swilled down beer after beer after beer, trying to wash away the uncomfort-able feelings I'd experienced during my brief visit to The Ark.

Finally, we slumped to the floor and let the music wash over us like breakers at the seashore. As I lay there, memories of the night in Canada, when I'd seen my life flash before me, came flooding back to remind me just how close to the edge I really was.

The infamous Paradiso soothed me for a few hours, but when I awoke late the next morning at The Shelter—we'd arrived back very late and incurred the ire of the caretaker, who had to get out of bed to let us in—the sense of impending doom was even stronger.

We had to leave Amsterdam—right away!

Mac knew someone who lived in a small town not too far away; we could stay there until the money from the insurance claims finally arrived. It wasn't a perfect solution, but anything sounded better to me than another day in Amsterdam!

Our alternative accommodation arranged, I hung up the phone and stepped out of the phone booth. As usual, Central Station was bustling with people jockeying to catch trains and buses. We gathered up our bags and were set to head for a bus ourselves, when a voice called out: "Hi, remember me? I'm Sherry. We met last night at The Ark. Do you remember?"

I turned and there she was, smiling just as broadly as before, and not the least bit put out or uncomfortable about the fact that I'd brought our conversation to such an abrupt end by turning and walking away from her in mid-sentence. "Looks like you're leaving the city. What've you guys been doing, then?"

I grunted some non-committal remark, but Sherry wasn't deterred by my determined indifference. She told us how she'd only bumped into us because she had left her purse behind, and that she had been headed back to The Ark to get it when she saw us. "You must at least let me buy you all a hamburger and a cup of coffee before you leave Amsterdam."

Before we knew what was happening, we gathered up our bags and followed Sherry to the city's flea market. All five of us squeezed around a small table in a crowded cafeteria.

Perhaps it was the offer of a free meal, or perhaps it was the infectiousness of Sherry's cheerful, warm, and open personality that had drawn us. I wasn't sure, but here we were, huddled around a small table, having lunch with the very girl we had rudely snubbed the night before; the very girl who had unnerved me so much. I bit into my hamburger, thinking how confident this young lady was to trust herself to the company of four rough-and-ready customers like us—and I envied her composure.

We made small talk for a while before she asked again: "So what brought you here to Amsterdam?"

We fixed our stare at the table and chewed silently for a few moments. Finally, I decided to tell her straight. I swallowed and cleared my throat. "Well, Sherry, we're traveling through to the East. We've set out on a journey to find God."

I waited for her laughter, but it didn't come, not even a snicker. Quite the opposite, she seemed genuinely excited by what I had told her. So I shared with her about our experiences and conversations, Alan, Gary, and Mac chipping in when they thought clarification was needed. Together, we brought her up to date on our spiritual quest: "...and so we're on a kind of pilgrimage, if you like, to discover God."

Sherry was the first person who hadn't dismissed us as cranks. Rather, she seemed to identify with what we were saying, and spent the next two hours telling us of her own search for God, for truth, for meaning, and how it had been resolved when she found "the Lord."

Here was a kindred spirit, someone who understood, someone on the same journey as us. My excitement grew as she spoke. Then suddenly, it was dashed. She began telling us how she was a Christian, a disciple of Jesus; that He was God and that she loved Him. "How sad. She's fallen for fairy tales and falsehoods," I thought as she talked on. I had left such fairy tales and falsehoods locked in St. Patrick's, and I wanted nothing more to do with them.

We drank more coffee and continued talking. Despite her misguided spiritual quest, Sherry's vivaciousness still engaged me. Finally, she announced that she really had to go. However, if we weren't doing anything in the evening, we could join her for supper at The Ark. It would be fun, she told us, to talk some more.

Our eyes followed Sherry out of the cafeteria. The four of us seemed to have fallen in love with her. All at once, we began to chatter about this incredible girl: someone who was really interested in us, who recognized the longings we had inside, who didn't laugh at us, who wasn't afraid of us, who accepted us as we were—even if she was sadly misguided about God. We wondered what it was that made her like that.

None of us seemed to be able to put our finger on it. Still, we knew two things: we weren't leaving Amsterdam after all, and we had a date at The Ark.

10

Coming Home

The afternoon could not pass quickly enough. We had decided not to touch any alcohol or drugs; we didn't want to arrive at The Ark with our brains in orbit and sky-high smiles stretched across our faces. We respected Sherry too much to do that. Instead, we spent the afternoon talking, trying to decide why such a sweet and innocent-looking girl would take the time to befriend us.

As we talked on into the gray afternoon, I felt a deep-seated cautiousness inside. Sherry had identified my inner hunger, and held out the prospect of an answer to my deep longing. Yet I feared that when the answer presented itself, I would not be able to reach out and take hold of it. Such an act, my insecurity reasoned, would expose me and make me vulnerable and weak in the others' eyes.

If the bearded guy who seemed to stand guard over the door to The Ark had had a smile the night before, it paled into insignificance compared to the grin he flashed as we arrived at The Ark. His teeth gleamed as he welcomed us back. I tried to project an air of casual disregard, but it seemed to go unnoticed amid the welcome we were receiving.

Sherry met us with a gentle smile that conveyed she was glad to see us. She guided us across to the second houseboat, moored alongside. On board, we stepped down into a large kitchen area. In the center of the kitchen was a range stacked with sizzling fry pans and steaming pots. A team of long-haired cooks bustled around the cluttered kitchen, adding spices to pots and chopping vegetables into salads. There was an aura of peacefulness about these people that, combined with the appetizing smell of dinner wafting from the range, brought a strange sense of contentment to my heart. I couldn't understand it.

"This is the main dining room," said Sherry, as she led us through a door. A large table with space enough for about forty people to sit around it commanded the center of the paneled room. "We live on this boat—there are dormitories right below us. This is also where we invite people to come and spend time with us." Sherry guided us to our places at the table. We sat awkwardly, nervous about all the unfamiliar people who were arriving to take their place at the table, also. "This is Peter Gruschka. He lives on The Ark, too," said Sherry, introducing us to the young man who sat down by us.

For a moment, the room was filled with exuberant laughter and excited chatter as people filled each other in on the activities of their afternoons. Slowly, the hubbub began to die away, and as it did, my eyes automatically followed the gaze of everyone to the far end of the table.

I blinked my eyes to make sure I was really seeing what I was seeing. At the end of the table stood the tallest man I had ever seen. His six feet six inch frame, exaggerated by the low ceiling of the houseboat, towered above us, while his eyes surveyed those seated around the table. My eyes caught his glance for a moment. It wasn't a cold stare, but a warm engaging look that said, "Welcome, it's good to see you here."

As striking as his height was his clothing; a white baggy, Indian-style shirt and long, baggy trousers—white from head to foot. From where I sat, I could see that the color of his sandals matched his long sandy hair and beard. He immediately struck me as a larger-than-life version of the picture of Jesus that had hung in the living room at home.

"That's Floyd McClung. He leads the community here," Sherry whispered by way of explanation, as he began to speak. Floyd's voice was warm and reassuring as he welcomed everyone to The Ark, and then asked people to introduce their guests.

As people began to stand and introduce people around the table, I realized that the four of us weren't the only strangers. Finally, Sherry stood, introduced us by name, and told everyone how she had met us. I cringed in embarrassment, wishing I could just quietly slip under the table where no one could see me.

"Okay, let's give thanks," Floyd announced, once introductions were complete. He bowed his head, and as he did so, I noticed that everyone else followed suit. Out of deference to Sherry, I bowed mine, as well.

It took a moment or two before I realized that Floyd was actually praying over the food. It was the first time in my life that I'd ever sat down to eat and not just dived straight into the meal. It was an odd experience, and I wondered exactly what the point of it all was. Finally he finished, and the food was brought out to be served. Soon the air was once again filled with conversation and laughter.

The food was good, and free, so I piled my plate high. I concentrated on eating as a means of avoiding the questions and comments coming from those seated around us. With my mouth full, I could give only the briefest response, if any at all.

As they chatted and questioned, and as I chewed furiously on my food, I felt my old paranoia and feeling of insecurity begin to rise. I began to desperately wish that I had dropped some speed or downed a few beers before coming; that would have at least given me some of the confidence I needed to make it through the visit.

I felt strangely frightened and vulnerable—like a small boy on his first day at a new school. Yet Sherry, seated beside me, seemed confident and at ease. The contrast struck me: the world-weary man was unable to mumble more than a few words, while the youthful, naive girl was self-assured and calm. How could this be? What was missing? What did I lack?

My discomfort grew until, by the time the meal was over, I was desperate for a cigarette to calm my agitation. It had been more than an hour since I had smoked my last one, and my hand automatically made its way to the pack in my jacket pocket. I was just about to pull a cigarette loose from the pack when I looked around and saw that no one else in the room was smoking, and there was a conspicuous absence of ashtrays. I reluctantly let the pack fall back into my pocket.

No sooner was I resigned to not having a cigarette when books were passed along to all those seated at the table. Sherry handed me one of the brown-covered books, and I turned it over. Emblazoned across the front of the book in gold lettering were the words, *The New Testament*.

The tall guy, Floyd McClung, stood up again and

began reading from the book. Sherry turned to the page for me, and I followed the words curiously as they were read. Then he began to give a brief explanation about what he had just read. None of it meant a thing to me. He could have as easily been speaking in another language, because I had no idea what he was saying.

I was still trying to work out what on earth Floyd had been talking about, when I realized that most of the young men and women had started to sing. The words flowed easily—something about God's love. They obviously knew the words by heart, and looked around, smiling at each other as they sang. I wasn't sure whether I should laugh or hide my face in embarrassment, so, not knowing what to do, I stared at the top of the heavy wooden table, breathing a long, slow sigh of relief when they finally finished and dinner was over.

Everyone had a job to do, and no one seemed to mind. Plates and cups were gathered up and taken off to be washed. The table was cleared, wiped down, and the chairs arranged neatly around it. Through the door to the kitchen, I could see others busy at work washing dishes, cleaning counters, and putting things away. The whole operation was carried out so cheerfully that I could scarcely believe it was actually happening.

Sherry and Peter, the young man she had introduced us to, led Alan, Mac, Gary, and me over to some old armchairs grouped together in a corner of the room. We sank into the armchairs, the four of us looking at each other, puzzled, as Sherry and Peter began to talk to us about "the Lord," whose name had seemed to repeatedly pop up in the conversations around the dinner table. I nodded non-committedly, understanding little of what they were saying, and was relieved when they finally finished. We said thank you and goodbye, and before leaving, Sherry invited us to come back again.

I could hardly wait until we were outside before tearing a cigarette from the pack in my pocket and lighting up. I took several long, deep draws of the cigarette before I felt the nicotine begin to soothe me. We were full of questions about what we had just experienced, and began to bombard each other with them.

"What did you make of all that, Alan?" "Mac, have you ever seen anybody like the freaky tall guy with the white robes? And what about all this talk about Christianity—the only Christians I've ever met are hypocrites. Could there be some truth in all their talk of God and His love for the world?" "Of course not; how could anyone really have their act together and still believe in Jesus?" Our discussion went on late into the night. Contrary to our expectations, drugs and alcohol didn't seem to help shed any extra light on things.

Yet, despite all the awkwardness and unease I had felt while on The Ark, I came away with a strong sense in my heart that there was something in the atmosphere of The Ark that I couldn't live without.

So, the next evening—and every evening for the next week—we returned to The Ark. Each time I returned and saw their smiling, friendly faces, I was overcome by the same rush of insecurity, but it was mixed with the promise of something fantastic, something I couldn't put my finger on, but which kept drawing me back like a drug. It was a curious, paradoxical mix of something I couldn't stand being near, and something I couldn't bear being away from, either.

Eventually, my fuzzy mind decided it had the

answer—they were on something. McClung, the big fellow, the ringleader, had a secret supply of some kind of super drug stashed below decks. That was the answer; and I wanted—needed—some of it.

The following evening, soon after arriving at The Ark, I challenged Peter: "Come on, what are you all taking? What are you on? I know you're on something."

He looked at me with a chuckle. "Well, I guess if you put it that way, we're on Jesus. That's all!" he replied, clapping me on the shoulder, his chuckle turning to full laughter.

It wasn't the answer I'd expected, and I wasn't really sure what he meant. But I believed him. A gut feeling told me that he was telling the truth—whatever that truth was!

Throughout our visits to The Ark, Sherry and her friends continued to talk to us in broad terms about God and the world, and what we thought life was all about. They were stimulating conversations that we eagerly looked forward to; we hoped they might provide some understanding for us in our search for God. But, perhaps more compelling than these conversations was the intangible sense of welcome we felt every time we stepped on The Ark. These people were for real—we felt cared for.

Feeling this way, we jumped at the invitation to come live on board The Ark as part of the community. There was a great attraction for us in just being part of a group of people who really cared for each other, not to mention the prospect of further stimulating conversations about God. The Ark, we decided, would be the perfect place to stay and prepare ourselves before finally setting out for the East to really find God!

But before moving onto The Ark, we had business to attend to back in Nottingham. Alan, Mac, and Gary had been told by their insurance companies that their claims could only be paid out if they personally applied for them back in England. The final third of my claim was also awaiting payment there, with the same stipulation of appearing in person to claim it. With our money all but gone, we decided to risk a trip back to Nottingham for a few days to complete our swindle.

Back in Nottingham, I couldn't shake the impression that the people from The Ark had made on me. The four of us excitedly told Sarah and Jenny about these amazing people we'd met, and how they had asked us to come and live with them. Sarah and Jenny seemed to capture our excitement, and wanted to go back to Amsterdam with us. However, we decided we should ask permission first, so we agreed to call them as soon as we could after getting back to Amsterdam.

I faced another long interview with a claims investigator. Finally, when he seemed satisfied with my explanation, he handed me a check for the outstanding balance of my claim. However, he insisted I return the following day to complete a few formalities. Formalities! What formalities? There had been enough of them already.

A feeling of suspicion overcame me. They were on to my swindle, I was sure. If I came back the next morning, there was sure to be a police officer waiting to arrest me. I panicked: was it paranoia or reality? My mind couldn't decide, so I packed my bags, called the other three, and to their surprise, told them I was flying back to Amsterdam first thing in the morning.

As the plane dropped in on its final approach to

Schiphol Airport, I was frozen in my seat by an overwhelming sense of foreboding and fear. I broke into a cold sweat, my knuckles white as I gripped the arms of my seat. I was going to die in this Dutch city! I don't know where the thought came from, I just knew. I felt the drops of sweat slide down my neck and drip across my rigid back.

For the first time since childhood, I tried desperately to pray, searching my foggy memory for the words. *Our Father*, I stammered silently to myself. It was no use, I couldn't remember the words, and besides, I wasn't sure who I was saying them to. Paranoia, fear, foreboding, and insecurity swirled inside me like a hurricane as the wheels of the plane bumped onto the asphalt of the runway and the engines screamed in reverse thrust as we decelerated. My heart was still pounding as the plane pulled to a halt at the gate.

As I made my way toward The Ark, my excitement turned to apprehension. What if they had changed their minds and wouldn't let me in? After all, it had been several days since they had made their offer. Wrestling with my apprehension, I strolled aimlessly along the canals and through the narrow side streets of central Amsterdam. Finally, after several hours, I gathered enough composure to make my way to The Ark.

I knocked twice on the broad wooden door of The Ark. I waited anxiously for it to open. When it did, I was greeted by a big smile. "Hey, it's John Goodfellow, isn't it? Welcome back—come on in!" Anxiety turned to joy and relief as I descended the steps into The Ark.

Two days later, Alan, Gary, and Mac arrived back. Each had similar stories of suspicion to tell. They, too, felt like someone was onto their swindle. However, we were reassured by the fact that it would take the police a long time to trace us to these two big old houseboats moored at the back of Amsterdam's Central Station. If and when they did, we'd be long gone on our overland pilgrimage to the East in search of God. They would never be able to track us down!

All four of us were welcomed onto The Ark as part of the guest list. As it turned out, there were about a dozen of us altogether—outsiders who'd been invited to spend some time living on board.

It was explained to us by those who lived on board full-time that we were expected to fit into the daily routine of the community. The routine consisted of communal breakfast at 7:30 a.m., followed by two hours of jobs around the boat—washing, repairing, maintaining, cooking. Then, at mid-morning, everyone met together in the main room for what was called "Family Time." Family Time, which usually lasted a little over an hour, was a time when those in the community sang and prayed before Floyd spoke about what it meant to live as a Christian, and read at length from the Bible.

At first, these times were very intimidating for me, but as the days passed, I began to find them less awkward. While I didn't really understand what it was all about, I was happy to clap along to the singing, even trying to join in on the occasional song I had picked up from sheer repetition.

Floyd's religious talks all seemed a bit remote, and at times, downright boring, but I put up with them, because they seemed linked to something much wider and deeper—a thrilling, heart-warming, tingling sense of belonging and purpose that seemed to emanate from everyone who lived on The Ark. It was an infectious feeling that all those visiting The Ark seemed to feel, and although I didn't know what it was, I knew that it existed, and that I wanted and needed it for myself.

Occasionally in the evenings, the four of us slipped away for a few beers to brood over all we were experiencing on The Ark. But none of us could put our finger on it. What were we experiencing? While we couldn't understand it, we all agreed that for the first time in our lives, there was a pulse of real, hard hope beating.

I sat cross-legged on the floor, relaxing into the familiar flow of a Family Time song. It was a short, expressive song that seemed to be mirrored in the faces of those around me. I sat and watched the faces of those singing. There was a warm glow on them, but also an intensity; as though they were not just singing the words—they were expressing them to someone or something. For them, the song carried a deep and transcendent message, far beyond the simple song I recognized it to be. The atmosphere in the room pulsed with joyful and enthusiastic voices, accentuated by the accompaniment of hand-claps and bongo drums.

I listened intently to the rising crescendo around me. There was a warmth in it that I had not felt before, and I wanted to enjoy every aspect. As I listened, a symphony of additional voices—majestic and proud—suddenly seemed to have joined in with our small group. I began hearing the sound of thousands of other voices. It was the most beautiful sound I had ever heard.

But it couldn't be; I was on an old houseboat moored to a pier at the back of Amsterdam's Central Station, not in one of the fine opera houses of Europe, where you expected to hear such sounds. I shook my head and slapped my ears, but the sound continued. The sound wasn't just a ringing in my ears—I was actually hearing it. It was so clear and close that I assumed someone had switched on a tape player.

I craned my neck to see where the sound was coming from. But there was no audio equipment in sight. Everyone else was concentrating on singing, and didn't seem to notice anything out of the ordinary.

I was still wondering what on earth was going on when I was pitched face forward. I sprawled on the floor, and could feel something coming from deep within. Like a wave rolling across a bay, a flood of tears that cascaded down my face. The voices of the thousand hidden singers and those of the people around me ran together, and then were blocked from my consciousness as gut-wrenching sobs—spasms from the depth of my being— overtook me.

It was all happening so fast and unexpectedly; it was almost as though I could stand back and watch it happen. I couldn't control it; I couldn't stop it. Tears flowed down my cheeks and dripped onto my shirt. Intermingled with the sobs were great gasps of anguish.

What will everyone around you think? my mind seemed to say. But I had no time to contemplate the thought. A great flood of emotion had burst forth from the core of my being. But it felt strange—as though the release of all these pent-up tears and emotions was washing everything away and leaving the real me deep inside.

With this washing away, I saw myself as I really was, for the very first time. Selfish, arrogant, spiteful, vicious, uncaring, proud. What I saw frightened and revolted me. I saw how I had hurt, robbed, cheated, lied, abused, and damaged those around me. I remembered a hundred justifications that I had made: they won't miss the money; she's been asking for it; he's hurt me; I needed it. Whatever truth may have been in them was no longer important; they were all part of the blackness that was my life. My anguish was great. There were no excuses; no one to blame but me. There was nowhere else to turn with a finger of accusation. From top to bottom, I was rotten, filthy, and wicked.

But as I saw myself as I really was, I was aware that the tears, sobs, and gasps of choking emotion that I was experiencing were also washing these things from me. I could feel those years of self-justification, deceit, hurt, and excuses being washed away.

I continued to weep uncontrollably, but the embarrassment was gone. In its place was a sense of relief and welcome: "It's over; I don't have to pretend any more." My tears were purging the blackness from my life.

I became conscious of the singing around me once again. I looked across the floor at Floyd. His eyes, with their reassuring warmth, met mine. He gently reached into his pocket and pulled out a big white handkerchief, which he passed to the person next to him. Hand to hand it came around the room to me, and I pressed its pure, fresh cleanness against my tear-streaked face. I looked back at Floyd in a gesture of thanks, and he smiled a smile of understanding. It was as if he knew exactly what I was experiencing, and yet was saying that he accepted me without question.

Someone put their arm around me in a gesture of acceptance. "It's okay, John, we understand, we understand," they said, as my sobs began to subside.

I wished I understood. All I knew was that what

I was experiencing had everything to do with the very essence of my life, but I couldn't explain it.

The understanding of what I had experienced began to come in the days that followed. Many of the things Floyd had talked about began to slowly take shape in my mind. I started to understand what he had been saying. Also, Peter and a number of others from The Ark community began to talk more directly to me about God and His world.

God had created man in His image, they told me. God had intended the world to be a beautiful place of harmony and peace where He and His creation could enjoy each other's company forever. But through willful disobedience, man had rebelled against God's order, which in turn had created a separation between God the Creator and the beings He had created.

According to the Bible, this separation meant that no one was perfect, that every person on earth—through sin—had gone wrong. To correct this situation, God sent His Son, Jesus, into the world to "pay the price" of our wrongdoing, and reunite us with God. God's penalty for sin was death, but Jesus, who had lived a sinless life on earth, was crucified, taking in His body the punishment we deserved because of our sin.

But the story did not end there. Crucified and buried, Jesus had risen from death, and in so doing, had defeated the power of sin once and for all. All that needed to be done now was for people to believe and understand that Jesus' death and resurrection were done for them, and experience freedom from sin and the old patterns of their life. This was the "new birth," and was the beginning of a spiritual odyssey that stretched on for eternity.

Only God's Holy Spirit, they explained, could help people understand these things. Indeed, they told me, it was the Holy Spirit who was at work in my life, breaching the dam and allowing years of walled-up emotions to flood out during Family Time. Not only that, but since I'd arrived at The Ark, they had been praying for such a thing to happen.

Gently and carefully, they laid the whole picture out for me. The more they explained, the more I could see a whole new world opening before me. I was eager to discover more about this world, so during the course of long conversations, I learned how I could apply to my life the things they were telling me.

But there was one catch. Even though I accepted all they told me about Jesus—that He was fully God and fully man at the same time, that He was still alive, because He had risen from the dead, and that He would live forever at the right hand of God—I just couldn't bring myself to believe that God had created the world in the first place. That step was too much for me—until one morning when Alan, Mac, and I were out putting our bricklaying skills to work.

We were building a wall around the waste-water pipes at the rear of the boats. The three of us busied ourselves digging the trench, laying out the site, and setting the bricks in place. It was then that it struck me just how easy it had been for us to construct something. We had made plans, followed them, and as a result, a brick wall was taking shape. I carried this simple logic over and applied it to God: If we—created beings—could design and make something, then surely a supreme being—God—could design and make a world.

Standing on top of the half-built brick wall, understanding pulsed through me like a lightening bolt. "That's it! I understand!" I exclaimed out loud. Gary, standing below watching our progress on the wall, looked up at me with a puzzled look on his face. "I believe, Gary, I believe! God *did* make the world!" I shouted down at him. He continued staring at me as I dropped my trowel, jumped off the wall, and ran inside. "I know it's true. I believe!" I shouted as I ran in.

Below deck, in my small dormitory room, I knelt beside my bunk to pray. "Oh, Jesus, I know You're real," I began, the gray winter water of the Ij lapping against the outside of The Ark, inches from my head. For the second time in my adult life, I was praying—only this time, I knew someone was there; I believed!

"God, I'm so sorry for all the dreadful things I've done in my life...." I continued on as I slowly and methodically began to lay out my misdeeds. Peter had told me during one of our conversations that becoming a Christian meant confessing your sins, and I didn't want to miss confessing a single one. It took more than an hour before I had confessed every sin I could remember.

Finally, I asked Jesus to come into my life: "Jesus, I believe You are the Son of God, and that You died to take away my sins. I believe You can forgive me and give me a new life as Your child. Please come into my life right now. I have made such a mess of my life so far, I want You to take charge of it. Please help me. I have hurt so many people in so many ways. Please change my heart, and take away all the anger and bitterness I feel. As You have promised, make me a new person. I want what it is you've given all the others here on The Ark."

I finally stopped talking, and slumped forward onto my bed. I felt a calm, secure peace rippling through my body. I felt clean and new—my prayer had been answered!

I knelt by my bed in the cold, damp belly of The Ark for a long time, enjoying the sweet, gentle feelings that had flooded into me.

Finally, it was dinner time, and I stumbled excitedly to the dining room. I gulped my food, all the while trying to disguise my huge smile. I managed to keep my secret until the meal was over, at which time I jumped to my feet and announced the words I'd heard several times before from other visitors to The Ark, but which had always mystified me: "I've been born again!"

The dining room erupted with cheers and shouts of congratulation. People applauded, and others gently slapped my back in a gesture of congratulation, acceptance, and support. Then the room filled with singing as everyone started to praise God. For the first time since coming to The Ark, I was able to join in and really feel part of it.

Like a traveler who had been away for a long, long time, I had come home—and coming home felt great!

11

First Steps

The warmth of the welcome still burned in my heart as I slipped below deck. On my bed lay my jacket, and my hand automatically reached out and pulled a pack of cigarettes from the pocket. It was my ritual; my after-dinner smoke. As I slid a cigarette from the pack, it hit me that things were different—something truly dramatic had happened. My hands were acting out of habit, but inside, I had absolutely no desire for a smoke.

It wasn't that I thought I shouldn't, it was just that I no longer wanted to. For the first time in more than twelve years, I had absolutely no desire to draw nicotine into my lungs. I turned the pack of cigarettes over in my hand, pondering what was happening. Everything had happened so fast, and it was all so new that I realized I hadn't the faintest idea how my newfound faith would affect my lifestyle.

I made my way up on deck. It was a chilly night, but I felt warm and comfortable on the inside. I turned the pack of cigarettes over in my hand a few more times, staring curiously at it, still pondering all that was happening in my life. Then, with a flick of my fingers, I sent the pack tumbling into the gray water of the Ij.

I watched it float on the surface for a couple of minutes before it filled with water and begin to sink. As it sank, my desire to ever smoke another cigarette sank with it. I was free! There had been no pain of withdrawal. It was as though someone had anesthetized me and surgically removed it from my life. What had once been such an important part of my life was gone!

It didn't take long before I realized that the same thing had happened to my desire for drugs and alcohol. I was lying on my bunk one evening when one of the other visitors to The Ark whispered that we could slip into town and score some dope or have a few beers. Normally I would have jumped at the opportunity, but this time, I simply had no desire to go. The desire had been taken from me. Perhaps more than the smoking, this about-face was remarkable, since I had been addicted to both alcohol and drugs for some time.

Whatever operation had been performed to remove these things from my life was more surely a transplant than an amputation. In place of my desire for smoking, getting stoned, and drinking was a new desire to absorb as much of the Bible as I could. The passages that I'd heard read and discussed in the previous weeks came flooding back to my mind, and I desperately wanted to read them for myself.

I began poring over the Bible, often for two hours or more at a stretch. I was captured by what I was reading; suddenly it all made sense to me! Words that had once been distant and detached were now of crucial importance. My heart raced with anticipation every time I picked up one of the well-thumbed Bibles that lay around The Ark. It was as though I had a personal stake in all that was written there.

So much of my life had been spent in a fog of confused thoughts and emotions, but now there was clarity. Things began to make sense, and I knew that a change of momentous proportions had taken place in my life.

Some of the men who worked on The Ark began to help me explore what this change was, and what it meant. We spent long hours discussing how becoming a Christian wasn't just about turning your back on an old life, but embracing a whole new one. They explained that God had a plan for my life that He wanted to unfold for me if I would let Him.

It had been three days since I had stood and made my dinnertime announcement of my conversion; three days in which so much in my life had changed. I sat late into the evening, talking with two new friends at The Ark. I thrilled to what they told me; Jesus was coming back again—soon. According to them, the Bible teaches that Jesus will one day return to earth, and everyone will recognize Him as the sovereign Lord of the universe. No one will be able to deny His majesty and authority. It sounded so exciting to me, and I sat listening to everything they had to say.

Then it happened again—another "wave" crashed over me, doubling me forward. But it was different this time. Instead of a rush of gut-wrenching emotions bursting forth from deep within, this time something washed over me. Like perfumed oil starting at my head and running down over my body, it came, warm and luxurious. I basked in the moment. It was as though liquid love had been poured over me.

The richness and tenderness of what I was feeling reduced me to tears. Deep sobs began to surface, but this time I gratefully welcomed them. The previous time, I had been unsure of what was happening, and how I should respond. This time, though, I just sat and enjoyed the liberation and freedom that came with being able to weep unashamedly. My heart was melting inside me, responding to the encompassing warmth of love I was experiencing. Layers of indifference and selfishness were falling away from me in the face of God's care and concern. It was a glorious moment; one of those moments you never want to end.

Then, with my head bowed, still enjoying the sweetness of the moment, I sensed someone standing above me. Jesus. His wounded hands were outstretched and welcoming. No words were necessary on my part as He spoke directly to my heart: "John, you belong to Me now. You are Mine. I accept you and I love you. John, you are Mine."

I treasured the words a moment, and then the awareness of this powerful presence left. In wonder and thankfulness, I wept quietly. I knew I needed God's forgiveness for the evil I had done in my life. Now I knew He had granted it, for no other reason than He loved me, totally and selflessly. I knew I would never forget the wonder of that moment.

My friends sat by quietly as I was immersed in God's love. Finally, I raised my head and looked at them, my face beaming. One of them reached over and threw his arms around me. I held him with genuine affection. I was glad to share this moment with someone. As we embraced, the tears still rolling down my cheeks, I realized the change that had come over me. For the first time I could remember, I felt comfortable sharing my emotions with someone else. I felt loved and accepted; I was part of a family that really cared for me—God's family.

Somehow, late that night, I made it down to my bunk and drifted off to sleep in a warm haze. The next morning, I awoke long before anyone else, the intoxicating awareness of God's accepting love still with me. I wrapped myself in my thick coat and clambered up on deck. Wisps of mist floated above the water, and an icy wind blew in from the North Sea across the low-lying Dutch countryside. I felt its refreshing sting against my cheeks as I paced the deck. "I love You, Jesus. I love You," I whispered over and over. It felt so good to say it; so liberating.

There was no letup in my excitement in the days that followed. I reveled in the newness I found in everything. Ordinary, everyday things like rainstorms and food became a source of fascination and delight to me. God was behind them all. Nothing happened by accident; everything was part of God's marvelous plan in shaping the world. It was as though I had previously only seen things in black and white. Now I was seeing everything in glorious technicolor; the mundane had suddenly became magical—a whole new world had opened to me.

Finally, several days later, Gary made his own private peace with God, and was born again. What a joy it was for us when two weeks later, the two of us, joined by six others, were baptized in a small chapel located on one of Amsterdam's back streets. The congregation at the chapel knew the work of The Ark well, and often allowed their baptistry to be used to baptize new converts. First, we gave a short account of how our lives had been irrevocably changed by the power of God, then we were lowered beneath the water and raised up to jubilant singing and clapping.

One of those who witnessed the event was Peter Gruschka. In the weeks I'd been at The Ark, we had developed a close friendship. At first, I was indifferent toward him, but since the night I knelt beside my bunk and asked Jesus Christ inside my life, our relationship had warmed. Since becoming a Christian, I found myself responding to people in a different way—Peter was one of those.

Peter was tall and rangy, with cascading curly hair. To look at him sitting in the crowded coffee bar of The Ark, you would have thought this easy-going German was one of the visitors, rather than a member of the staff. He had all the trappings of the typical dropout, only he had rejected the drug and sex scene in favor of what he had found in Jesus.

Before coming to The Ark, Peter had been a professional actor and singer, touring Europe in the cast of the musical *Hair*. This production was the ultimate statement of the peace and love culture, and shocked audiences with its full-frontal nudity and glorification of drugs and anarchy. During performances, cast members not only shed their clothes, but stepped down off stage to hand out marijuana to the audience.

The show had become Peter's life—until one night in Basel, Switzerland. As he and a musician friend were leaving the theater after finishing a show, they were met by two women waiting for them. The women asked if they could talk for a few minutes, and proceeded to tell Peter and his friend about how Jesus Christ had come into the world to rescue them from their sins and give them a wonderful new life. When the two women finished, they handed New Testaments to the two astonished men.

Both men were greatly moved by the encounter, and both later became Christians. They began to share their new faith with other members of the cast, and it wasn't long before gospel tracts and New Testaments were being handed out in the theaters, instead of marijuana. Finally, Peter was asked to leave the show—his Gospel message wasn't compatible with the show's New Age mysticism. So, with a burning love for God in his heart and an intimate understanding of others like him, he soon found himself working on The Ark.

I loved to hear Peter tell his life story, for it challenged me with what God could do in my life.

I was so overwhelmed by the newness of everything, that I almost forgot there was life beyond The Ark. Then I remembered: I had arrived at The Ark on the run from the police in England. This was one of the many things I was going to have to sort through, now that I was part of God's family.

I thought the best way to start was to talk to Floyd. He listened silently as I sheepishly told him that I'd come to live on The Ark under false pretenses. I filled him in on the details of the story. I knew that what I had done was wrong, and apologized for misleading him and the community. Floyd didn't seem at all disturbed by what I had told him. Rather, he was much more interested in what I was going to do next. He explained that it was up to me now. I had decisions to make.

As we talked, he opened his Bible and read a passage from it which said that when a thief became a Christian, he should pay back all the money he had taken, and then live a peaceable life.

Back on my bunk, I flipped through the pages of my Bible until I finally found the passage Floyd had read from in Ephesians chapter four, and read it for myself. *It's pretty clear what you've got to do, John*, I thought as I reread the passage. The following morning, I sought Floyd out again.

"I've decided, Floyd," I told him. "I believe I should go back to England and confess to all the things I've done wrong, and try to put them right."

Floyd nodded, "I think you're right, John." There was a warm, reassuring smile on his face. Later that afternoon, we biked over to the insurance office where I had made my false claim. As we pedaled along, Floyd seemed oblivious to the strange looks people were giving him as this long-haired giant went by. At the office, Floyd strode in to explain on my behalf why we had come.

The man behind the counter listened impassively to Floyd, while at the same time eyeing me up and down closely. He said he remembered me, and knew my claim had been fraudulent, because detectives had recently been in to interview him about it.

"Well," I began, "three weeks ago I became a Christian. I know what I did was wrong, and I plan to go back to England to confess to it, and I want to pay all the money back."

He was clearly surprised at my openness, and after he he wrote down a few details, Floyd and I turned to leave. "I've never heard anything like this before in my life," he said, shaking his head with a smile as we reached the door. "Good luck!"

I knew it wasn't a matter of "luck." I had tangibly felt God's love and now, in return, wanted to demonstrate how much I loved and cared for Him by putting right my past mistakes. This seemed like a good place to start.

But not all my wrongs had taken place out in the streets; a good many of them had taken place within the four walls of the Goodfellow household: bitterness, jealousy, resentment, and anger. I badly wanted to break down this history of hurt, and allow my family to see the exciting new life I had discovered. I wasn't sure where to start, but I finally decided that perhaps it should be with a phone call.

The line was crackly, but it was good to hear Mom's voice. I hastily told her that I had met some great people; that I had become a Christian, and was coming home to sort out a few things.

"What do you mean, Johnny?" Mom sounded confused. "I don't understand. The police have been around here looking for you. What've you been up to? You're not in any trouble, are you, son?"

"It's okay, Mom," I tried to explain. "I've become a Christian. These people here are going to help me. Everything's going to be okay. Honest."

"What do you mean, you've become a Christian, Johnny? You've always been a Christian, son. Your father and I took you to church for years. What are you talking about?" She sounded anxious and a little baffled.

I wasn't sure where to begin. It was obvious that this revolution in my life was not going to be easily explained over the phone to my family. "I know I went to church for years, Mom, but I never knew Jesus. But now I've met Him. He's alive!"

With Mom still confused as to what I was talking about, we ended our conversation. My heart ached to be able sit down face to face with them, and explain what had happened to me.

There was another phone call I needed to make. I pulled some more coins from my pocket, and deposited them into the money slot. I waited for the dial tone, then slowly and deliberately dialed the number I had written on a piece of note paper. I waited a moment for the number to go through, then I heard it ring. "Nottingham Central Police Station," a matter-of-fact voice answered on the other end.

It was soon obvious to me that it wasn't every day that someone called up from overseas to admit to a crime they had committed, and arrange to come home and face the consequences. Eventually, though, I was able to speak to someone in the Criminal Investigations Department who knew of my case. We arranged the details of when and how I would travel home. Officers would be waiting in England to arrest me as I stepped off the ferry.

Surprisingly, the next few days were a blur of happiness and anticipation. I felt as though all the Christmas Eves of my youth were rolled into one: those wonderful hours of expectancy while lying in bed, knowing that something wonderful was about to begin and wishing it was closer.

I spent my waking hours reading the Bible, and asking a million and one questions about this new life I had begun. I sat alongside the members of The Ark community in the coffee bar in the evenings. I listened as they talked to visitors about Jesus, desperately wanting to join in the conversations, but always being too embarrassed at what these streetwise skeptics might make of my bungling attempts to describe my new faith.

I stopped outside Central Station, the spot where it had all begun. It was hard to believe it had been only a few short weeks, so much had happened. Gary, Mac, Alan, and I had been planning to leave the city and begin our pilgrimage to find God, but a young lady who had forgotten her purse changed all that. We had been so determined to set out to find God, when all along He was more concerned about finding us. What a strange turn of events it had been.

Now, here I was on my way back to England to

face the consequences of my past. My euphoria began to evaporate as I approached the platform and saw the train waiting. But having Peter Gruschka standing beside me was reassuring. He was a tangible reminder that I wasn't alone in this situation. I had been overjoyed when he volunteered to accompany me back to England and support me through the things I would face. He was a shining example for me of the selfless love of God that I had seen lived out in the lives of those who followed Jesus.

Every fiber of my being told me that God was with me, so I sat down and waited for the train to depart. I felt some anxiety about what lay ahead, so I reached for my Bible to read. It was funny that in such a short space of time, the Bible had begun to feel so at home and satisfying in my hands. I had found the Bible to be fascinating, exciting, confusing, shocking, and enlightening all at the same time, and I enjoyed every moment spent reading it.

I still wasn't too sure of my way around the Bible, so it was with no design on my part that I found myself reading from the book of Isaiah. As I read, the passage seemed to spring off the page at me: "When you pass through the waters, I will be with you...you will not drown....Fear not, for I will be with you....I have called you by name."

With a jolt of assurance, I accepted the passage as a message of support from God for the trip I was about to undertake. "Thank You, Father God, for giving me this encouragement," I prayed quietly to myself as the train began to move.

As the English coastline came into view, I felt my heart begin to pound. Questions about what would happen once we arrived flooded my mind. I could feel my stomach tighten, and once again I reached for the security of my Bible. I expectantly thumbed through its pages until once more, I found myself in the book of Isaiah. "Don't dwell on the former things...I'm making a way in the desert," the passage read, and I felt the knot in my stomach loosen. I didn't know what was going to happen. I didn't know how God was going to work. But I knew everything would be fine; God was in control!

My confidence in God continued to grow as the ferry docked at Harwich, and as I made my way down the gangway, I was almost delighted when I saw the policemen waiting for me at the bottom. Indeed, so warmly did I greet them that anyone watching could easily have mistaken us for long lost friends!

At Harwich Police Station, Peter and I were viewed with some suspicion to start with. I was taken to an interview room, where I made a full and detailed confession of my fraud to a detective. As I spoke, he wrote everything down in longhand, and after I had read over all he had written and signed it, I was set free on bail, to await further contact from the police back home in Nottingham.

The train rattled along, each mile bringing us closer to Nottingham. I felt a curious mix of nervousness and excitement growing in me. How were my parents going to respond to the homecoming of the son who had made the name of Goodfellow a cruel joke for so long?

12

Putting Right the Past

I was bursting with excitement. I had no doubt that my family would see the change in my life. I brimmed with confidence—not in me, but in the amazing person I had discovered: Jesus Christ. He had forever changed my life. I had known no peace in my life until the day I met Jesus. Now, where there had been no peace, there was a deep, solid, and tangible peace.

I paused a moment before rapping on the old wooden door. Those who had the most reason to remember the old John Goodfellow with regret would see the difference. I was certain of that. When they saw the difference, I could explain the how—or, rather, the who—of my transformation. For the first time in my life, I felt a love for my entire family. I wanted to respond to them in gentleness, instead of the hardness and coldness of earlier times.

The door creaked and swung open. Mom stared at me a moment before I engulfed her in an uncharacteristic hug. She was surprised, but pleased. I moved on to embrace the rest of the family, as well. It felt so good to see them and touch them. Things felt right, I was responding out of genuine love and affection for them.

Soon we were all nestled around the table, sharing a noisy dinner. I began to tell them of all that had happened to me. However, from the nervous glances I was getting, I sensed it was too soon to share it all. I held my peace, and enjoyed Mom's home cooking; there would be plenty of time later to share everything. As we continued with dinner, I found myself blinking back the tears as I looked at my family seated around the table.

Their faces were so familiar, but it was as though I was looking at them through different eyes. I was seeing them in a softer light. No longer were they people who, I felt, only wanted to squash me down. Instead, they were people with needs, hurts, wants, and pains of their own. There was Dad: tired, proud, self-reliant, and lonely. Mom: weary, worried, cheated of the close family she had so longed for. Joan: eyes dull and old, her hopes of enjoying a glamorous life crumbled by single parenthood. Trish: in so many ways a typical teenager, but with a fiery streak of anger—so much like I had been.

"Oh, Jesus, I love them so much," I whispered under my breath. "Thank You for letting me see my family as You do. Please let them see You in me."

The meal over, I hung back in the kitchen making small talk with Mom as she busied herself cleaning up the dishes. I helped her make hot drinks for everyone, which I carried through to the lounge, where Dad and the girls sat watching television. I sensed the moment had come.

An awkward silence invaded the room when I asked if I could switch the television off for a few minutes, because I had something important that I needed to share. They shuffled and twisted as I pulled up a chair to face them, breathing a silent prayer for God's help. I then proceeded to bring them up to date on all that had happened to me.

"First, I want to say that I'm ashamed of being, for so long, the worst son you could have wished for. I've hurt you and embarrassed you. I've dragged the family name through the mud. I know I've been a disgrace to you all." I sat quietly a moment, watching their faces.

"But I want you to know that three and a half months ago, I became a Christian. I began a personal relationship with Jesus Christ. I asked Him into my life, and He has forgiven me for all the wrong I've done. He lives in my heart, and has completely changed my life. I want to live for Him for the rest of my life." I took a breath. I had so wanted to communicate the passion I had in my heart that it had all come out in rush.

We had never been a family that shared our emotions—except perhaps for anger—and opening my heart in this way was something completely new. My story had created an uncomfortable silence.

Finally Mom broke the silence. "Johnny, it's wonderful to have you home again, son, but I don't understand. You've always been a Christian. I'm glad you've decided to calm down a bit now, but...." Her words trailed away, revealing her utter confusion at what had happened to me.

"Mom, it's not a matter of having gone to church in the past," I replied desperately. "It's that God has changed my life. Jesus has set me free. He has made me a new person."

Trish broke the moment by getting up and turning the television on again. The strained silence was washed away by the dialogue of a soap opera.

I left them watching television, and slipped upstairs to my old bedroom. Inside, the door closed behind me, I fell to my knees beside the bed and began to pray for each member of my family by name. I pleaded with God to reveal Himself to them through the Holy Spirit, in the same way that He had broken into my life. Although initially discouraged, I was sure deep inside that it was only a matter of time.

Peter Gruschka was able to stay in Sarah and Jenny's apartment while they were away. The apartment was just a few hundred yards from my parents' home, so Peter and I met together each morning to spend a couple of hours praying and reading the Bible. These were important times for me. They were times when I drew heavily on Peter's knowledge and guidance. As we prayed and studied together, I could feel my love for God growing stronger and stronger.

Even before Peter and I met in the mornings, I had usually spent an hour or so in prayer by myself. I rose early, before anyone else in the house, made myself some coffee, and settled into a comfortable chair with my Bible.

In the afternoons and evenings, I often wrapped myself in a heavy coat and made my way down to the end of the street, where an open tract of land ran down to the edge of the River Trent. I walked up and down the river bank, singing under my breath and praying for my family, my old friends, and my future as I did so. When the occasional cyclist or walker passed and gave me a strange glance, I didn't care—I was so happy.

Before arriving back home in Nottingham, I had determined to reinforce the change in my character through my attitude. It wasn't hard to do; I'd been such a poor example of a son in the past that any change for the better was quickly noticed.

In addition to getting up early every morning, I spent most evenings at home. I never went down to the pub as I had in the old days, preferring instead to stay home and read quietly in my room, or watch TV with the rest of the family. I continued to quietly ask God to touch my family powerfully and personally with His love.

Joan was the first. It was my first Sunday home, and the rest of the family, except for Joan and her baby son, Sean, were out. A former airline hostess, Joan had gone through a number of relationships before becoming engaged to be married. Then she had become pregnant, and the marriage plans fell though.

She had come home to have the baby, and was now trying to pick up the pieces of her life. But she was struggling. Tranquilizers and chain smoking were what seemed to get her through the day. This person whom I had always resented as tough and self-possessed was now vulnerable and desperately needy. It hurt me to see what had happened to her.

The house was quiet as I sat down and began to tell Joan, in a little more detail, all that had happened in my life. She seemed interested, so I kept on going, telling her how Jesus wanted to transform people's lives, if only they would allow Him. I told how He wanted to forgive all the wrong that people had done, and take away their hurts, filling them with peace, joy, and hope that defies description. I knew it was all true, because it had happened to me.

As I talked, Joan burst out: "I know it's all true! When you sat us all down the other night and began to speak, I just knew that God existed. I don't really know how to explain it, Johnny, but I just knew, deep down, that what you were saying was true. I believe it...and I know it's what I've been looking for all my life. What should I do?"

I explained to Joan how she needed to admit all the wrong things she had done, and ask God to forgive her. Then she needed to ask Jesus into her heart as her Lord and Savior, and when she did that, He would come in—no doubt about it.

Joan sat on the edge of the sofa and began to pray, falteringly, following the pattern I suggested. As she prayed, she began to weep, finally slumping to the floor where she cried aloud, long and hard.

My heart somersaulted with joy at what was happening. I wasn't sure what to do as she lay on the floor beside me crying, so I began to pray, also. I asked God to answer her prayers and give her His new life.

I don't know how much time went by, but eventually Joan's crying stopped, and the tears dried. She knelt and looked up with a beautiful smile of peace on her face and began to whisper: "Thank You, God, thank You. Thank You, Jesus, thank You. This is what I have been wanting for so long."

When she finally stood up and looked into my eyes, I could scarcely believe it. Her face was visibly softer, and it almost seemed to glow. In her tear-smudged eyes, I could see the sparkle of real happiness. We hugged each other tight. I buried my head on her shoulder and murmured: "Thank You, Father God. Thank You!"

In addition to the heaviness that lifted from Joan's features, her anxiety also left that afternoon. She quickly discovered that she no longer needed tranquilizers or cigarettes to calm her nerves.

In the days that followed, Joan and I began meeting together in my room to read the Bible and pray.

It was so wonderful to share my limited spiritual knowledge with another young Christian who was as enthusiastic and hungry to learn as I was.

When we told the rest of the family what had happened, they seemed unperturbed, dismissing it all as over-emotionalism. Everything, they assured us, would be back to normal after I'd been home a few weeks and things had had time to settle down.

Trish didn't seem to understand what was going on. She was a fashion- and music-conscious teenager, who thought her older brother and sister were going through a religious phase; that it was something we would come out of; it wouldn't last. I sensed she was keeping a keen eye on me, watching secretly to see if I made any mistakes.

Several weeks later, though, she agreed to go to an evangelistic rally at Nottingham's Albert Hall. The speaker was Nicky Cruz, the tough New York gang leader who'd been saved through the remarkable ministry of David Wilkerson. His story had been told in *The Cross and the Switchblade*, and I was eager to hear this man whose life, in so many ways, mirrored my own.

Joan and Peter came along as well, but somehow we got separated from Trish and her young friends, and didn't see them again until we were on our way home. I noticed Trish sitting a few seats in front of us on the top deck of the bus. I called her name, and she turned to flash me a broad, excited smile. I knew she had met Jesus. "Thank You, thank You, thank You," I softly repeated all the way home.

As the weeks went by and the home Bible study group grew to three, my parents began to relax a little. They didn't like to talk about what was happening in a direct way, but they could see it was bringing a peace, closeness, and happiness to their children, and that made them happy. Unfortunately, not everyone felt that way.

One evening, after visiting relatives, Mom came home distressed. It was obvious that some harsh words had been exchanged about this strange new religion I had brought into the house. This was a new kind of faith. What about the Catholic Church? Nervously wringing her hands and chewing her lip, Mom took off her coat and walked into the living room, where she promptly burst into tears.

"My life's falling apart. I'm losing all my children, and we're falling out with the rest of the family. What's happening here? I just don't know what's going on anymore. You've got to help me, John," she pleaded.

I looked into her aching eyes. "I can't, Mom. Nobody can. Only Jesus."

Suddenly she changed tracks. "I want to be like you and the girls, John. How do I get what you've got in your lives?"

"You've got to invite Jesus into your heart, Mom. That's all. Just turn to Jesus."

Collapsing into a chair, she said that she wanted to do that right away. I went over, put my arm around her, and led her in a short prayer, asking Jesus to forgive her for the times she had failed, and to come into her life. As we finished, she jumped to her feet. "It's gone, son; it's gone. The burden is gone. All the guilt's gone; I feel lighter!" She exclaimed with delight.

Mom stopped drinking right away.

If Dad felt threatened by this latest transformation in his family, he said nothing. By now he was an old man, with only a hint of the steel he once possessed. He was officially retired, but had a part-time job at a local pub, and spent most of his time puttering around there or in the back garden.

I felt so sorry for Dad. He was trapped by past hardness and bitterness. I longed to be able to reach inside and help him. He allowed me to start saying a brief prayer for us all before meals, and together, we worked silently and contentedly in his garden. He said little, but I could feel his approval of the changes he was seeing.

Mom, the girls, and I continued to pray for God to touch Dad's heart.

We had just finished our Sunday lunch after attending morning service at church. There was a quiet, peaceful contentment about the house. Mom, Trish, Joan, and I had grown close to each other and to the Lord. It was as though God was allowing us to make up for lost time.

We were still chatting around the table when we heard the kitchen door open. It was Dad, back from his Sunday drinks at the pub. By now, Dad was a shadow of the man I used to hate and fear in equal measure. I longed to be able to get through to him. I so wanted him to find what the rest of us had found. As I heard Dad plop down in a chair in the kitchen, I heard a voice inside say: "Go into the kitchen and tell your father the Good News of Jesus Christ."

I had come to trust this inner voice as the prompting of God's Spirit. So I left the dining room table and walked through to the kitchen, where Dad was sitting on a chair, his head slumped in his hands on the table. He looked so old and tired as he looked wearily up at me before letting his head slump back into his hands.

"Dad, the Lord has told me to come in here and share the Gospel with you. This is the word of God to you. It's the first three verses of Isaiah 61." I read, "The Spirit of the Lord...has anointed me to preach good news to the poor...to bind up the broken-hearted, to proclaim freedom for the captives...."

I closed my Bible and looked straight at Dad as I began to speak freely and effortlessly. For almost ten minutes, I boldly told Dad about the Good News of Jesus, and the hope He offers. I shared with Dad as if I was addressing a crowd of hundreds, and could sense a special authority and power in what I was saying. Dad sat, head still in his hands, as though he wasn't hearing me.

As I finished, he looked slowly up at me. There were tears in his eyes. It was the first time I had ever seen him weep without a bottle in his hand. These were real tears, and the sight of them wrenched me inside. Dad slowly dropped from the chair to his knees. I rushed forward and knelt beside him on the cold linoleum. I put my arms around him, and the rush of emotion I felt was warm and good.

"Son, what shall I do to be saved?" he croaked out.

"Dad, ask Jesus into your heart. Here, like this...." We stumbled through a short prayer together, and spent a long time just holding each other with tears in our eyes.

The rest of the family came into the kitchen, and we held each other and wept in a way that once would never have been possible. God had made us a new family, and together we thanked Him.

Setting broken family relationships right had been my primary focus since arriving back in Nottingham. But there were many other loose ends that needed to be taken care of, lest they entangle me in my new life. In addition to praying for God to move in the lives of my family, Peter and I asked God each morning for help in knowing the way ahead in all the other things that still needed to be set right.

Within a few days of my return home, Gary, Mac, Alan, and I were reunited. They had made their way back to Nottingham during the previous weeks, and like me, had given themselves up to the police, with the express intention of putting things right.

We were still fairly close, despite all we had gone through together, yet those crossroad days in Amsterdam had also driven a wedge between us. Gary had committed his life to Christ, and was following his own plan for sorting out his life. Mac had told me shortly before leaving The Ark that he believed everything that had been said about God, but he just didn't want to act on it. Alan, after failing to persuade me to go with him, left The Ark in a hurry one evening.

Now, back in Nottingham, the four of us continued to meet together with Peter to study the Bible. In effect, we picked right up where we had left off in the searching, discussing, and exploring which had been a feature of life on The Ark.

I was distressed, though, by Alan's continued skepticism. He and I had been the closest. He was the one responsible for focusing my search for meaning in life on the spiritual realm. Through that realm, I had finally found what I was looking for. Now I was anxious that Alan make the same discovery, yet all the hours we spent reasoning and talking together didn't seem to be moving him any closer to making that discovery.

Upon arriving back in Nottingham, Alan had found work as a truck driver, and since I didn't have a job, I often accompanied him on his trips. We sat in the cab of his truck and continued our discussions.

One day, while driving back from Leicester to Nottingham, I became frustrated with Alan's unwillingness to accept what was so obvious. I found there were limits to my newfound patience.

I turned impatiently to him and said, "Alan, we've talked enough now. That's it. Give your heart to Jesus, man. Come on—you know it's all true! Don't be stubborn. Let's do it now. This is too important to waste any more time over!"

It was an outburst of deep concern, but I wondered if perhaps I had pushed too hard. All was quiet for a moment, then Alan looked at me and said quietly, "Okay, John, let's do it."

He pulled the truck off the highway into a country lane, and stopped about a hundred yards down. Alan switched off the engine and bowed his head over the steering wheel. I led him in a short prayer of confession and invitation for Jesus to come into his life. Beaming, Alan sat up and then jumped down from the cab and began to shout at the top of his voice: "It's really true, John. I believe it, you know!"

He fell to his knees on the grass as I climbed down to join him. "Look at the trees," he shouted happily, as the tears started to roll down his cheeks. "God made them, didn't He? God really made them! Oh, it's fantastic!" Alan's stubbornness and fear had finally been swept away, and in their place was a joyful effervescence.

Looming on the horizon was our forthcoming trial. I had been freed on bail to appear at Nottingham Crown Court five months after my return. Knowing that we were facing it together gave the four of us strength and encouragement.

We had already been warned that the charge— conspiracy to defraud—was very serious. The fact that we had committed other crimes almost certainly guaranteed prison terms, despite our willingness to help the police as much as we could.

When the detectives had interviewed me on my arrival back in England, they had not asked me if there were any more offenses I had committed. If they had asked me, I would have willingly confessed to my other crimes. But since they hadn't, I was left with a catalog of outstanding offenses that still needed to be dealt with.

During this time, a Bible passage from the gospel of Luke made a deep impression on me. The passage was about Zacchaeus, a tax collector, who became a disciple of Jesus. Upon doing so, he immediately declared his intention to repay all the debts he had incurred. In short, he wanted to put right all the wrong he had done. It was a free expression of his gratitude to God. I felt the same way. I talked and prayed with Peter about the best way for me to do it.

Finally, one morning, after spending about an hour in prayer, I sat down with a pen and paper and made a list of all those from whom I had stolen. There was the jewelry store where I had committed the "smash and grab" robbery; the bank where I'd run up a large overdraft; the insurance companies I had conned out of bogus sick pay while self-employed; the fashion shop where I had obtained clothes on forged credit; and the money secretly pocketed at the Crazy Horse Saloon and the Swiss hotel...the list went on and on.

Then I began making a list of all the individuals I'd hurt both physically and emotionally. I tried to remember all the names of the people I had battered and bruised. I jotted down the names of all the women I had wronged through my selfish relationships. Sharon's name headed the list.

My wrist ached, but I continued to scribble down

names. Peter and I had prayed that God would help
me to remember every last small matter, and as I
wrote, more incidents kept flooding into my mind.
The money I owed on taxes from my self-employed
days; the muggings and thefts.

At last, it was finished! I looked at the lengthy
list, wondering if I could really go through with it.
Remembering was the easy part...now I had to do
something with this catalog of selfishness.

13

Back on the Streets

"Johnny's back, and he's got religion," was the word on the street. Having been a part of Nottingham's underside for so long, it wasn't long before word was out.

Most of the old faces I encountered had heard that something had happened to me in Amsterdam; that I was different, or at least claimed to be. They were wary of me, and held me at arm's length. However, whenever a chance presented itself, I used it to make a stumbling attempt to explain what had happened to me that tearful night on The Ark.

One night, I drifted into the Flying Horse, looking for Cupe—one of Nottingham's well-known tough guys, and a man I had admired greatly. The Flying Horse, as usual, was smoky and noisy. I squinted through the cigarette haze, and spotted Cupe sitting at a corner table with some friends, laughing and drinking freely. I approached the table and sat down next to Cupe, greeting him as I did.

"Now then, Johnny, how's it going?" he asked brightly.

"Great, Cupe, great," I replied. "Maybe you've

heard. I've become a Christian."

"Yeah, that's right. Word's gotten around. What's it all about, then?"

As Cupe spoke, there seemed to be a spark of genuine interest beneath his rough-and-ready exterior. I began to tell him hesitantly about all I had been through. As I did so, he turned to his drinking friends, and with a wave of his hand, snapped at them, "Quiet down, will you! We're trying to talk here." They did, and Cupe and I spent the next twenty minutes talking.

Cupe seemed interested in all I had to tell him. As we talked, I reached into my pocket and pulled out a copy of Nicky Cruz's autobiography, *Run Baby Run*. "This is for you, Cupe," I told him, as I handed over the book. Before leaving home, I had scribbled a brief inscription inside the front cover of the book. "To Cupe: we've both traveled a hard road," it read.

Curiously reading the inscription, Cupe's eyes filled with tears. I pressed on with the conversation: "I want you to know, Cupe, that coming to know Jesus has transformed my life. It's the most wonderful, beautiful thing you could ever imagine. He can do the same for you."

Cupe looked up, embarrassed and vulnerable. "I know, Johnny, I believe it," he whispered. Then, pulling himself together, he turned back to his friends and with a laugh, snapped back to his former self. "Well, thanks, Johnny, I'll read this some time," he said, getting up to order another drink.

I was disappointed that the moment had passed, but I was also delighted. Cupe had been eager to listen. I was encouraged to believe that many of my other friends would want to hear about God, if I persisted in prayer and awaited the right moment to speak. I began to look for opportunities to explain what had happened in my life. Those opportunities came thick and fast the day I set out on my trail to restitution.

Peter and I had decided that, if possible, it would be good for me to complete my journey of restitution in one day. On the day in question, I arose very early and spent two hours praying and reading the Bible before leaving for the bank—my first stop.

I pulled the cast iron gate closed behind me. It snapped shut, and I paused for a moment, one hand resting on the cold metal, the other fingering the list in my coat pocket. I felt apprehension, yet I knew what I had to do. I walked to the end of the road and crossed the already busy main street. As I approached the bank, my stomach muscles tightened.

I stopped by the curb for a moment, and pondered what I was about to do. What was I letting myself in for? What was I going to say? How were people going to respond? Would the manager call the police? The knot in my stomach tightened.

Then the idea struck me. I could simply crumple up the list in my pocket, throw it away, and forget about it. No one would ever know. Drop the paper and walk away. It would soon be swept up with all the other curbside garbage to become just another scrap of paper at the city dump.

But it wasn't really that easy. It would be simple to dispose of words scribbled on a piece of paper, but I could not remove what they stood for. I had made the choice, and needed to bring it to completion. So I straightened my tie nervously, took a deep breath, and pushed open the bank door.

I made my way cautiously to the counter. The bank had opened only a few minutes before, so there were no lines. A cheerful teller with a Monday morning smile spread across her face greeted me.

"Hello, sir, can I help you?"

"Good morning. Yes, please. I'd like to see the manager, if that's at all possible."

"Certainly. Could you please tell me what it's in connection with?"

Her request threw me for a moment. I hesitated. "Well, it's very confidential and important. It needn't take very long."

She gave me a puzzled look for a moment. It was all too obvious to her that I didn't belong in a suit and tie. My long hair and beard didn't fit the bill of the average businessman. She finally told me to wait a moment as she went over to an office at the rear of the bank.

The seconds stretched into minutes. My tie felt like a noose tightening around the growing lump in my throat. I was fighting the urge to turn around and walk quickly out of the bank. It still wasn't too late to forget about all of this!

Then the teller was back. With another smile, she opened the security door and led me to the manager's office. She knocked on the solid oak door with the brass plaque bearing the manager's name, then entered, leading me in.

Half-rising from behind his broad, dark, wooden desk, the manager greeted me with a smile. He was unsure of the purpose of my visit, and I could sense his nervousness as he shook my hand. He then gestured for me to take a seat. He sank back into his own chair, and assumed an executive air.

The moment had arrived. It was time to do what I knew I had to do. I stammered out the first few words.

"Good morning," I accompanied the words with my best shot at a confident smile. "Thank you for

agreeing to see me. My name is John Goodfellow...."
As the words started to flow, I felt as though a button
had been pushed inside me. A warm sense of security flowed through my body. Everything was going
to work out all right—I could feel it.

"...I don't know if you remember me or not, but
I was a customer of yours for several years."

The manager looked at me encouragingly, but
without recognition. His fingers stroked the side of
his desk blotter as he waited for me to continue.

"I want you to know that I have recently become
a Christian, and I feel that God has told me to come
to you today and to confess to the fact that I owe you
a lot of money."

His face registered confusion for a moment, so I
pressed on, sparing him the embarrassment of having to respond just yet.

"When I had an account here, I wrote many
checks with no way of meeting them from my balance, and then ignored all your letters demanding
repayment. I did it intentionally and deliberately,
with no thought of repaying you. I stole it all, in
effect. I'm very sorry about this now, and I want to
ask your forgiveness for doing it, sir."

The manager nodded slowly and silently, with a
confused look on his face. He didn't attempt to
speak.

I pressed on. "I want to pay back all the money I
owe the bank. I hope to start work very soon, and
will be able to mail the first installment to you in
about two weeks, if that's all right with you."

The manager seemed more nervous than I was.
He laced his fingers together before responding, and
then sounded as though he were completing a business transaction.

"Well, thank you," he said as he wrote down my

name and address. "That all seems to be in order. Fine. We appreciate your having come in like this, and I look forward to receiving your first payment before the end of the month. Thank you once again." He rose and escorted me to the door.

Within minutes, I was back out on the street, drawing in fresh air with relief and gratitude. With my confidence rising, I made my way to the next address on the list.

Before the day was over, I had visited insurance offices, the guild hall, the jewelry store, the tailors, and the list went on.

Some of the people had been very businesslike, others had been short with me—though no one took up my invitation to call the police. If they had, with my criminal case for conspiracy to defraud still pending before the Crown Court, it would have meant certain jail.

There were those, like the manager of the local insurance office, who had been warm toward me. He smiled when I told him about the false sickness benefit claims I'd made while I was self-employed. He had been unwilling to pay up at the time, and did so only under extreme phone threats from me.

"I never did believe you, you know," he told me. "So what's all this change of heart about?"

His genuine interest gave me an opportunity to talk longer about my loneliness and insecurity, the desperate hunt for meaning in life, and the incredible new life I had begun since meeting Jesus. As I spoke, he pulled me up short with a laugh. "I see you've already started trying to convert people, then!" he chuckled.

"That's right," I answered him, looking straight into his eyes with a smile.

"Well, I think your coming in here and owning

up is the most amazing thing that has happened to me in all my years in this business," he said with a shake of his head. "I wish you well."

At home that night, I added up all the money I had promised to repay. It amounted to several thousand pounds. Money I didn't have. But I wasn't downhearted. I knew God would give me the strength and ability to see it through to the end.

I soon found work back on the building sites, and I worked hard. Each Friday night, I brought my fat wage packet home, gave Mom some money to cover the cost of my keep, and saved a few coins for travel and an occasional cup of coffee. The following morning, I took the rest of the money down to the Post Office to convert it into postal orders, which I mailed off to pay my debts. Each week I dutifully checked off the amount in a small black ledger I had bought for the purpose.

I knew that going back to the building sites would be a real test for my new faith. But I was determined to make it clear from the very first day that I was a Christian.

When lunch break arrived, I headed over to the construction shed with my lunch box, already knowing what I was going to do. We all flopped around a table together, my fellow workers opening their packs of sandwiches and pouring coffee from their thermoses.

As they busied themselves, I purposefully bowed my head and said a silent grace—and I stayed in that position longer than usual, just in case someone had missed it. Then I looked up, and opened my lunch box. One of the men opposite me, Lenny, stared at me with a big grin.

"What's that all about, then?"

It was just what I had hoped for. "I was praying—

saying thank you to God for my food."

"Oh," Lenny guffawed, "that's all right, then. I thought you'd slipped into a coma."

I laughed with him, and the ice was broken. They knew where I stood now. Over the lunch break, Lenny began to ask me questions about what a Christian was, and I had a great opportunity to tell him about my journey of the past few years.

As I shared, the men never sneered at me or joked about my faith, as I had thought they would. Indeed, as time went by, they began to single me out to talk. They wanted my advice about what they should do in their relationships with women, or voiced their concern about a teenage son who was going astray. A few even asked me to pray for them, which I did—as well as for all those who didn't ask.

My exhaustive attempts to pay restitution also involved sending a number of letters overseas to people I had ripped off in my travels. Since I wasn't a great writer, writing these letters was particularly difficult. In due course, however, the replies began to filter back, saying there were no hard feelings, and wishing me well.

The toughest letter I had to write, though, wasn't about money. It was the one I sent locally—to Sharon. I had decided that it would be wrong for me to seek her out personally. So in a letter, as best I could, I told her all that had gone on and asked if she could find a way to forgive me for the terrible way I had treated her and ruined her life. I offered to meet with her if she wanted to, and told her that I would set in motion repayment of all the child support that for so long I'd refused to pay.

I never heard back from Sharon, and the silence was painful. I resolved to pray for her and for our daughter, whom I had last seen in a family snapshot when she was six months old. I prayed that one day, they would find it in their hearts to forgive me, not because I deserved it, but because they had found the love, healing, and wholeness that only Jesus can bring.

While I decided it was best not to try to make direct contact with Sharon, I did seek out a number of other women with whom I'd had fleeting relationships, in an effort to right incidents from my past.

In The Flying Horse one evening, I saw a woman with whom I'd had a brief affair, at the same time that her marriage—to a friend of mine—was breaking up. I went over to her and asked if I could have a few words in private with her. She was surprised to see me, but stepped out into the hall. It was an awkward moment. I wasn't sure where to begin.

"Look, Suzy, you'll probably think I'm crazy," I began, shifting uneasily as I spoke. "But I've become a Christian...."

"I know," she interrupted, looking at me uncertainly. "I've heard that you'd gone all religious, like. You're not going to lay any of that on me, are you?"

Things weren't going as I had hoped. "Well, I want to tell you I am sorry for having committed adultery with you, and want to ask you to forgive me if I caused you any hurt."

She bristled, obviously offended by what I had said. Her eyes flashed. "So what's wrong with a bit of sex on the side?" she retorted.

"Well, I'm a Christian, and I believe it's wrong to have sex with someone who is not married to you."

"Well, I don't!" she raged at me, as she turned to walk away. "I'm not sorry, and as far as I'm concerned, there's nothing to forgive, so you can just get lost with your Holy Joe stuff, mister!"

The encounter was over. I felt wounded and tender, yet I knew that I had done the right thing.

Finally, the day of the trial arrived. Mac, Gary, Alan, and I had all pleaded guilty to the offense, and an attorney from the small church we had begun to attend had volunteered to take on our case.

The four of us arrived at the Crown Court, having prayed for the strength to accept God's will in the matter. Indeed, I had already begun daydreaming about how I would start a prison Bible study if bad came to worse. Whatever the outcome, I had determined to make it count for God.

As we walked into the courtroom, we were greeted by our jubilant attorney, who announced, "God is already at work—they've dropped the conspiracy charges!" I was overjoyed. Dropping the conspiracy charge greatly reduced the seriousness of the offense in the eyes of the law.

When each of us finally stepped into the dock, we pleaded guilty to the charge, and waited as the prosecutor told our story. Then it was our defense attorney's turn, and he told the judge how we had given ourselves up to the police, and assisted them in clearing up the matter. He told about our experiences at The Ark, which had changed our lives so radically.

Within minutes, we left the courtroom, free men. We were each fined, ordered to pay costs, and given an eighteen-month suspended prison sentence. We hugged each other and our families excitedly, and thanked God for giving us our freedom.

The next day, the story of our transformation was splashed across Nottingham's evening newspaper for all to see. The judge described our transformation as remarkable. So remarkable, in fact, that it had prompted him to sentence us as first-time offenders, despite our previous convictions.

The evangelical church we had begun attending was also a great support to us throughout. It was a fairly traditional, middle-class church, but if the congregation had been shocked by the small band of enthusiastic young people who had appeared in their midst, they didn't show it. We felt accepted and loved by the church, and enjoyed attending Sunday services and the mid-week prayer and Bible study meeting.

Yet as time went by, and the number of new Christians from among our old circle of friends grew, we began to feel uncomfortable in the church. My heart burst to share the Gospel with people who were as lost as I had been, but evangelism wasn't a central theme of the church's life.

Sarah and Jenny returned from their time on The Ark, with their lives turned upside down by their encounters with God. They introduced me to Sarah's brother, Jamie, a young tailor. I befriended him, and it wasn't long before he became a Christian.

Eventually, a group of us began to meet together in Sarah and Jenny's apartment. Jamie and I led these informal fellowship meetings, which grew quickly. Soon there were thirty or more young people attending each week. There was such a mixture of people: new Christians from among our circle of friends and contacts, and Christians from other churches in the area who were looking for a deeper walk with God.

Even though it had only been a few months since I'd become a Christian, God seemed to equip me in an amazing way so that I was able to pass on all the teaching I had absorbed during my intensive time of study on The Ark. These mid-week meetings were alive with the presence of God, as the Holy Spirit moved powerfully, yet gently, among us. There were tears, laughter, prayer, and praise, all in an easygoing atmosphere that made newcomers feel at ease.

After one particularly moving time of praise and worship, I suggested we take the meeting out into the open. What would God do in our midst if non-Christians were around to witness it? The others agreed, and so the following Sunday afternoon, we headed into the center of Nottingham, to the square in front of the guild hall.

We nervously tuned our guitars, picked up our maracas and bongos, and began to sing praises to God, slipping from one short, happy song to another. Within minutes, we had attracted a sizable crowd of inquisitive afternoon strollers.

After about twenty minutes, we stopped and tried to engage some of the onlookers in conversation. It was a toss-up, however, as to who was more ill at ease in the situation—them or us. We finally made our way home, happy at how things had gone, yet frustrated. Something was missing, and we weren't sure what it was.

We repeated this pattern for a few more Sundays, until at the end of one session, I was approached by Ansell. Ansell was a short, wiry miner, originally from Jamaica, who usually preached in the square before we arrived.

Each Sunday, Ansell stood atop a concrete post, dressed in his smartest suit, and holding a Bible to his chest, shouted out how people needed God in their lives. I had seen him in action on a couple of occasions, and was immediately impressed by his bravery, while at the same time feeling intimidated by the negative reaction he received from some of those listening.

On this particular Sunday, Ansell had stayed to

listen to us sing, and, after we were done, singled me out. He smiled and thanked me for singing about Jesus so freely. "But, you know," he added seriously, "you've got to preach the Gospel. You've got to tell them how Jesus can save them. You won't see anyone converted by just singing. You've got to tell them the Good News!"

Deep down, I knew he was right, but the prospect alarmed me. What would people think if we did what Ansell did? Would they laugh at us in the same way? Were any of us brave enough to stand up and preach? At our mid-week meeting, we talked and prayed about what Ansell had said—and we agreed that he was right. We had to stand up and speak out. The only question was, who would do it?

All eyes turned in my direction!

The final song began to taper off, and I knew the moment had come. I was terrified, and breathed a silent prayer for help as I stepped up onto a wooden bench. I looked out cautiously at the crowd gathered to hear us singing and clapping. I wasn't sure what I was going to say, but it was too late to back out.

I raised my hand in a gesture of acknowledgement, and opened my mouth. As I did so, a flood of confidence surged through my body. It rose from my feet, welled into my heart, and burst out through my mouth. Suddenly, my mind was racing with thoughts and ideas, and the words fell unexpectedly and easily. They weren't timid words, but bold, confident words. Indeed, it didn't sound like me at all.

"You know," I began, "I never used to be up at this time on a Sunday! I used to stagger across this square dead drunk most weekends, and if I'd seen somebody doing what I'm doing now, I'd have thought he was completely mad!" I paused and smiled, and watched as some of the crowd turned and walked away. But others stayed and smiled back. The interest in their faces drew me on.

"You see that jewelry store over there?" I pointed in its direction. "I broke into that store one night: smash and grab. I got caught by the police further on down the street. I used to get into fights in that pub over there...." Again I pointed, and began to telling my story of drinking and fighting, of sex and drugs, violence and lostness. And Jesus. The words spilled out effortlessly. My fear was completely gone. In its place was an excitement I had never experienced.

As I finished preaching and stepped down from the bench, I tingled with excitement and satisfaction. Ansell had been right: there was power in preaching the Gospel. I felt as though I had been plugged into an electrical outlet. I wanted to do it again and again.

Buoyed by the response of people to our first public preaching, other members of the fellowship took their turn over the next few weeks. I was eager to give them an opportunity. I found myself looking forward to these Sunday afternoon meetings with delight and excitement.

I was always nervous when my turn came, but once I stood and opened my mouth to speak, God seemed to fill it with authority, clarity, confidence, and love. If any of those who stopped to listen wanted to talk further, we sat down and spent the rest of the afternoon talking to them, or we invited them to our Tuesday night fellowship meeting.

Soon, there were a number of people who had become Christians through our street meetings. The number of people attending our weekly fellowship meeting grew to over forty. God's love was being shared with family, friends, and acquaintances, and they were responding.

Wherever possible, we tried to encourage new-comers to become involved in a regular church, but many felt more of a closeness of the presence of God in our Tuesday night meetings than in the more formal Sunday services they were attending.

As winter approached, fewer and fewer people stopped to listen to us on Sunday afternoons. We felt less and less enthusiastic about being out there in the biting wind. So during winter, we shifted our focus more solidly to prayer and Bible study.

Within just a few months, we had a thriving, growing fellowship made up mostly of young and new Christians. I was confident that God was en-abling me to cope with the demands of running the fellowship—I certainly knew that I didn't have the resources within myself.

But I also began to worry about the future. I wasn't sure that our young leadership could con-tinue to run things forever.

Over the months since my return, I had kept in touch with The Ark through a series of lengthy let-ters, advising them of my spiritual growth and all that was happening. I asked them to pray about the fellowship, and in reply, Floyd suggested that a cou-ple from The Ark come over to join us and assist in leading the fellowship.

We were all delighted at the idea, and in due course, welcomed Paul and Mary Miller into our midst. They were an American couple who had be-come Christians while following the hippie trail in India, and had subsequently spent several years working on The Ark.

It was a brave move for the Millers. They arrived in gray, cold Nottingham, knowing little about what they faced, and finding themselves living in a tiny one-room apartment. I relinquished formal leadership of the fellowship to Paul and, along with Jamie, acted as his assistant. Under the gentle guidance and direction of the Millers, the fellowship continued to grow and flourish, both in the numbers attending and in the knowledge of God's love and power in our lives.

Those were busy days, bursting with an ever-deepening love for God and the wonderful, exciting new life He had given me. My joy was full as I experienced the closeness of our newly-united family. I took the opportunities that presented themselves on the building sites to talk about God, began to see my debts being paid off, and soaked in all the new things I was learning in the fellowship.

Then, one day, a dark shadow was cast across our family.

I was working on a building site in Meadows, right across the street from where we had lived when my cousin attacked us with a knife. I hadn't been at work long when my heart began to spasm. I went cold inside.

"Home; you've got to go home." I knew God was prompting me, so I threw my tools into my bag, dumped them in the construction shed, leaped over the wall, and ran down to the bus stop, shouting back over my shoulder to my work mates that I had to go home urgently.

Arriving home, I was met at the door by a distraught Trish. "It's Dad, John. There's been an accident...."

The story soon unfolded. Dad had been knocked down by a bus, and had suffered serious head injuries. He was in the intensive care unit at the hospital. Joan, Mom, and I fell into each other's arms, and prayed for God's help to be strong.

Two days later, Dad died without ever regaining consciousness. We wept together. We had only been close as a family for a few short months. It almost seemed cruel.

Yet, through our grief, we could see a test of our faith. We knew that if we weren't careful, we could easily become negative toward God for having allowed this tragedy to happen.

But as we wept, mourned, and comforted each other, we agreed together that we could trust God. Though we didn't understand it fully, we knew there was a reason for things happening the way they had.

Our tears of grief were mixed with tears of thankfulness for God's goodness in allowing us the days we had enjoyed together as a family. We began to see how different it was to face death with God in our lives. Even in the sadness of Dad's death, there was a sense of hope for the future.

For Joan, that future began several months later. After I had left The Ark, it became part of Youth With A Mission, an international missionary organization with operations all over the world. They had also expanded their work in Holland.

While still keeping The Ark going, Floyd and a group of the "Arkies" opened a training center at a farm called Heidebeek, in the picturesque village of Heerde, sixty miles north of Amsterdam.

Joan made contact with this new training center, and with her toddler son, Sean, had gone off to Holland to attend a Discipleship Training School: a school where young Christians were given a strong grounding in their faith before entering full-time Christian service of one kind or another.

To see Joan take this step was like the frosting on

the cake for me. I thanked God at every turn for His
goodness to our family.

14

Plenty to Learn

As we packed into Sarah and Jenny's small apartment to praise God and study the Bible every Tuesday evening, I often remembered how, only a matter of months before, I had been staying in the small room upstairs, frightened of living and scared of dying.

Now life was a joy, free from fears, and death held no sting for me at all, only the hope of being with Jesus. It was such a turnaround. Every day was now an adventure in living for Jesus, and the prospect of being with Him forever was almost too much to contemplate. I eagerly looked forward to Tuesday evenings.

Saturday morning was another time I looked forward to. There was an exhilarating sense of satisfaction in walking down to the Post Office to mail off my bundle of payments. There was great joy in knowing I had completed another week's work, and could make a new entry in my ledger; the tangible record of my determination, with God's help, to put past things right.

Most of all, I looked forward to the Sunday afternoons when we gathered to sing and preach in the center of town. The electrifying buzz of adrenalin that had surged through me the first time I stood to preach always returned every time I took my turn to address the crowd. I knew that that was how I wanted to spend the rest of my life. As soon as my debts were paid, I intended to commit myself to full-time evangelism.

For a short period, I actually joined Paul Miller in a full-time program of street preaching near Nottingham's main shopping precinct. We spent the mornings praying together, and the afternoons taking turns to preach and talk to shoppers and other passersby who paused to listen and chat. This experience only whetted my appetite for full-time evangelism. I returned to bricklaying, more determined than ever to pay off my debts as soon as possible so I could get involved in the ministry to which I knew God was calling me.

I had been working hard and steadily in Nottingham for two-and-a-half years, and although I'd made a large dent in paying off my debts, it was frustrating how far I still had to go. I began looking for a faster way to pay off my debts.

Then one day, I came across an advertisement for bricklayers needed in Germany. The company seeking bricklayers was offering better wages than I could earn in England. Perhaps, I thought, this is God's provision for me.

I calculated that if I worked non-stop for six weeks, I could come home with all the money I needed, compared with at least a year's work in Britain. I followed up on the advertisement, and almost before I knew it, found myself in a small German town not far from the Dutch border.

Arriving at the station, I discovered that there were several other British bricklayers waiting to be picked up. Memories of my time in Canada flooded back, but I shook them off. I had been trying to master my own destiny in Canada, and had failed miserably. This time, God was firmly in control.

After being picked up by the site manager, our first port of call was the nearest pub, where the others immediately ordered a couple of beers each. My request for a cola raised some eyebrows, and I was able to spend a few minutes telling them why I had turned my back on drinking.

The site manager offered to drive me over to the hotel so we could discuss a few final details. On the way, I asked him what arrangements had been made for my tax payments.

He laughed as he looked over at me.

"What's so funny?" I asked.

"You've got to be kidding. We don't pay tax!"

"What do you mean?" I asked, trying to downplay my rising sense of panic.

"It's all cash in the hand. No tax, no questions. In fact, nobody really knows we're over here doing a job. We're sub-contracted to somebody else back home. A pretty tidy set-up, eh?"

My heart sank. I hadn't even gotten as far as unpacking my bags, and it seemed as though the whole arrangement was falling apart. "You mean it's black money, then?"

"Well, yeah, I suppose—if you want to call it that," he replied, shifting uncomfortably in his seat. "But everyone does it, you know. It's just the way things are."

"Maybe," I cut in. "But not me. One of the reasons I'm here for the job is to pay off the money I owe the tax man. I can't work on this basis. I'll have to go back home."

The site manager stared at me with a mixture of annoyance and amazement. "You've got to be kidding! It's good money down the drain. What are you, some kind of weirdo or something?"

"I'm a Christian," I explained. "I've given my life to Jesus, and He wouldn't want me to do this. I'm sorry."

With that, he turned the car around, and we headed back to the station. It was an uncomfortable few minutes' drive, as he spent the time trying to justify his actions, explaining it was part of the system. Nobody really lost out; the government wouldn't miss a few hundred pounds. I never answered him.

Standing in the brisk German air outside the station, my bag slung over my shoulder, I sagged on the inside. In just a couple of hours, my carefully made plans had fallen apart.

I was confused and disappointed. I knew that somehow, God had it all under control, that there was some sense to be found in it, but at that moment, it was beyond me. I needed some time to think and pray the matter through to see what God was trying to say to me through it, so I decided to travel over the border to Heidebeek.

It would also be good to see Joan. She had completed her Discipleship Training School, and had stayed on to become part of a ministry house in Epe, a village near Heidebeek. She and Sean loved the environment—the love of the people and the beautiful country setting made it a haven of peace.

I arrived in Heidebeek unexpectedly, but to a warm, enthusiastic welcome. Later, over coffee, Floyd McClung and I began renewing our friendship with warm hugs and smiles. I told him about my hopes and dreams, and how they seemed to have collapsed. He looked at me thoughtfully.

"John, why don't you stay here and go through our Discipleship Training School? There's one starting next week."

I knew from past experience that Floyd had a way of making the most outrageous idea seem matter-of-fact, but this one seemed too far out—even for me. My future was mapped out, and studying the Bible in the Dutch countryside was not part of it.

"I've got to work. I need the money. You know I haven't finished paying my restitution yet!" I sputtered.

Floyd didn't flinch. He smiled. "Well, why don't you just go away and pray about it, and ask the Lord if this is right or not? If it is, then He will provide for you, John."

I was already certain that I knew what the answer would be, but out of respect for Floyd, I agreed to pray about it.

As I prayed, a simple picture filled my mind. I saw a series of different doors that seemed to represent the ways open to me; avenues I could explore to pay back the hundreds of pounds I still owed. As I gazed at them, they closed—firmly—one by one.

Finally, there was only one door left open, tucked away at the side of my mind's eye, and above it was one word: *Heidebeek.* Through the open door, I was flooded in a bright welcoming light. It was like warm sunlight, the sort you just want to bask in. I realized that God was speaking clearly to me: He did want me to attend the Discipleship Training School (DTS). If I left to go home, I would be acting in disobedience.

I didn't understand it all, but I knew what I had

to do.

"Floyd, you're right," I told him excitedly. "I've prayed about it, and I believe the Lord wants me to stay here and attend the DTS." Floyd smiled one of his knowing smiles.

Heidebeek seemed a million miles from Nottingham. Instead of rising to start work on a noisy building site, I was able to enjoy the morning sun as it filtered through the trees in a haze of glorious color. Just to walk in the woods and listen to the sound of distant farm animals was peacefully refreshing. I saw immediately why Joan had been so attracted to the place.

As I walked to the main building for the first class of the DTS, I realized the mistake I had made in narrowing God's plan for me into a specific pathway. I had decided that there was only one way to do what He wanted me to do, and that was to work my debts off. I'd become so determined to do what God wanted me to that I had failed to recognize the fact that He wanted to help.

I was beginning to understand that there were other possibilities. There was still a long way to go in paying back my outstanding debts, not to mention my DTS tuition fees. So something far beyond my best efforts was needed; that much I understood.

My phone call home to explain my change of plans had caused bewilderment, so, anticipating some letters from the rest of my family, I strolled across to my mailbox. There was nothing there—except an envelope with no stamp on it. I opened the envelope, and out fell sixty pounds in folded notes. Tucked amid the notes was a scrap of paper with two words on it: "With Love."

It took several moments to sink in, and then I felt

the tears. I was deeply touched that someone gave me such a blessing. But even more, I was overwhelmed by the love of God that prompted them to do it.

As I stood there, the sixty pounds still in my hand, I realized that I was learning another lesson. I had been so determined to do the right thing and clear the debts myself, that it had almost become a matter of pride. I was going to do it. I was going to put things right.

But God seemed to be saying to me, "No, not that way, John. I've forgiven you. I love you. You don't have to try to earn that love through repayments. Thank you for your commitment to doing what you should—but now, I want to meet you halfway."

And He did. The envelopes were there each week as the DTS continued. Sometimes there were ten pounds in them, other times thirty, even once, two hundred pounds. They were always neat and tidy, and always anonymous, except for a note of love or encouragement. There was always enough to enable me to continue my repayments and pay the school fees, as well as a little left over to buy a cup of coffee.

There were times when I felt guilty about it. Why would God provide the money in this way, when I could just as easily earn it? Then I remembered that it was because He loved me; because He wanted to; because I could never justify or deserve that love. I needed to stop worrying, and embrace all He wanted for my life.

It had been nearly three years since I'd become a Christian. In that time, my life had been turned upside down. I had learned so much in those early days on The Ark, and had continued to grow spiritually back in Nottingham. I had seen my family and friends come to experience saving faith in Jesus, and that had fueled both my love for Him and my hunger to share the Gospel with others.

But God wasn't finished with me yet. There was still much refining and polishing He wanted to do in my life, and the quietness and tranquility of Heidebeek provided the opportunity for Him to do just that.

During the months of the DTS, I learned that there were still secret hurts and insecurities deep inside me which needed to be dealt with. Through times of prayer, teaching, counseling, and ministry with staff and guest speakers, I experienced a deep, cleansing work of the Holy Spirit in my life.

I still found it difficult to relate to other people. In the past, I had covered this difficulty by using drugs and alcohol. In the DTS, I was forced to face it and work it through. Although I was still somewhat of a loner, avoiding the snack bar during coffee break in preference for being on my own, I could feel changes beginning to happen.

I arose early in the morning, before the duties of the day, and enjoyed uninterrupted time alone with God. I wrapped a thick blanket around my shoulders against the early morning chill, and strolled out into the pre-dawn woods, where I spent time praising God, praying, and mulling over the Bible.

At night, I devoured the biographies of Christian pioneers such as William Booth, the founder of the Salvation Army, and William Carey, the missionary pathfinder. I was excited by what God was able to achieve through these men. I fell asleep at night, praying that one day God would use me in a similar way.

The more I grew in my relationship with the Lord, the more clearly I could see that success in the

Christian life depended, to a large degree, on the choices I made. I had to choose to walk in God's way. I had to accept the things He wanted to give me. In effect, God's love could only work as far and as deep in my life as I was prepared to let it.

Such understanding helped me come to terms with the way our old gang of four had dispersed in the days following our Amsterdam turnaround; we had all pretty much drifted apart after our court appearance.

Mac never made a commitment to Christ. Back in Nottingham, he had told me that he believed all he'd heard and seen on The Ark, but just wasn't interested.

Gary, who had followed my tearful steps to Jesus a couple of nights later, had returned to Nottingham with a desire to tell his old friends what had happened. He went after them in the pubs and clubs, spurning the offer of beer, and settling for pop instead. He sat down and told them about Jesus.

In fact, Gary was so anxious to go out and tell others about Jesus that he didn't want to "waste time," as he put it, meeting with Peter and me to pray and study the Bible. I slowly began to see less and less of him.

Finally, I spotted Gary in a pub having a beer. On the next occasion it was a couple of beers, and soon, he was right back into his old ways. An awkward shrug was the only explanation he could offer when I had the opportunity to talk to him.

Alan's situation was perhaps the most difficult for me to understand. We had been through so much together. He had been my closest friend, and I was so excited the day he prayed for Jesus to come into his life.

Then Alan's inner struggle had begun. "I know

that being a Christian means giving up chasing women, and I don't know if I can do that," he told me. My attempts to encourage him that God had a wonderful plan for a man and woman—but in the proper context of a committed marriage relationship—just seemed to go over his head. Eventually, he also turned his back on God.

Along the way, each of them had made choices that led to their current situation. Now, of the four young men who had set out in search of God, I seemed to be the only one who had found what he was looking for.

My stay at Heidebeek had taught me so much more about the wonderful God I served, that I was anxious to get out on the streets to tell others about Him.

As the end of the DTS approached, I was expecting to return to Nottingham to start preaching full-time with Paul and the other members of the fellowship. But Floyd had other plans, and when he asked me to stay on as a staff member and assist with the next school, I knew it was right for me to do so.

Being at Heidebeek also helped me to work out a new way of relating to women. Since becoming a Christian, I had been freed from the crude, selfish, disposable view of the opposite sex that I'd had since my early teens.

But even though those twisted attitudes had been torn from my life, in their place was an awkwardness and uncertainty in relating to women. I had not had a girlfriend in the last three years. I never looked for one, and instead, filled my life with a passion for God. I found Him to be all I wanted or needed.

I gradually found myself relaxing in the company of the female staff and students. I was able to treat them like my sisters, and I enjoyed the freedom that it brought.

But I was still shocked when one morning, as I strolled through the grounds during my prayer time, I sensed God speak to me in His gentle, quiet, assured voice, "John, the girl for you will be in the next school."

It sounded totally absurd, but I knew that it was God's voice I had heard.

15

Terry

As I scanned the group of newly arrived DTS students, I knew my life would never be the same. I fell hopelessly and wonderfully in love with Terry Gray at fifty paces. One glance at her set off a chain reaction that sent me reeling inside.

I was sure everyone could see my cheeks flush. I was desperately uncomfortable with what I was feeling. I was so self-conscious that I turned and walked away, as though I had an important errand to take care of elsewhere. I needed time alone to think.

I was still busily working through what it meant to be a new man in Christ. I had committed my life to telling others about Him on the streets. Having these feelings for a girl the first time I laid eyes on her was not in my plans; it hardly smacked of the spiritual maturity and solid faith I was longing to see grow in my character! I somehow managed to regain my composure before being introduced to these newcomers.

My role as a staff member in the DTS involved sitting through class with the students and encouraging them to work through and apply to their lives all the biblical teaching they were receiving on discipleship and God's character. In addition, we were there to support and befriend the students, and generally ensure that their time in DTS was a time of personal growth, where the foundations for future service were laid.

I was also put in charge of all the maintenance programs at Heidebeek—everything from changing a light bulb to laying the foundations for a new service road. If it needed to be made or repaired, it was my job to see that it got done.

But despite my thirst for Bible knowledge, and the rich discoveries I had made during my own DTS, I found it hard to concentrate and apply myself the second time around. Like a sailboat in a strong wind, my thoughts kept veering off course. They were soon followed by my eyes as I turned casually to sneak a glance at the young woman who had thrown me into such secret turmoil.

Concerned that no one pick up on my inner confusion, I made a point of avoiding any real contact with Terry, other than the occasional times when I sat and shared coffee with a group of students. I spent long periods alone with God, reading His word and Christian biographies. But always running through my mind were thoughts of this young lady.

I pieced together the little information I had been able to glean about her from overheard conversation. Terry was twenty-one years old, and came from a respectable middle-class home in the southern U.S.

She had become a Christian in her early teens, and had been called to missionary service in Europe at age sixteen. A French and Bible student, she had gone on a summer ministry trip to Europe with a group from Wheaton College. It was then, during a brief stopover at The Ark, that Terry had met Floyd

McClung. Floyd had told her about a Youth With A Mission community along similar lines to The Ark that was to be opened in France, and now she was at Heidebeek, preparing to go on staff in France.

Terry was trim and attractive, with long, auburn hair parted down the middle, dark brown eyes, and a ready smile. Her personality matched her good looks. I soon learned that her open, easygoing nature and warm sense of humor made Terry popular among her classmates. I often heard her bright peal of laughter rising from a group of students talking together or playing board games in the evening.

I was paralyzed around Terry. The few times I spoke to her, I felt tongue-tied and clumsy, and was sure she had dismissed me as awkward. I told myself that it was crazy to feel this way about someone I hardly knew, especially in light of my past.

She was a nice American girl from a good background who, without so much as a hiccup, had gone from attending Sunday School regularly to having a powerful and personal walk with God. By contrast, I was a rough-edged Englishman from the slums, who had experienced nearly every forbidden thing there was to experience before my life caved in. Oil and water were a better match than we were, yet I couldn't get her out of my mind.

It was a daily struggle. Everything I was striving for seemed to be called into question. All I had dreamed of in serving God was close at hand, and I was finding it hard to concentrate because I was mooning over a girl!

The ministry at The Ark had always been based on what Floyd called "friendship evangelism"— gentle, caring, low-key, and long-term. Floyd had seen too much "plastic preaching," and believed many of the young dropouts with whom he came in contact would be completely turned off by a direct approach. So workers from The Ark set out to win people's hearts through friendship—and then talk to them about Jesus. It worked—I was living proof!

Yet a powerful urge welled inside me to tell strangers about Jesus: those who may never have the opportunity to be befriended over a period of time, or those who needed a more direct challenge to their lives. Many travelers were already disillusioned with life—that's why they were on the road. But others didn't think there was anything missing from their lives—they needed to be challenged. We had seen it work time after time in Nottingham. I had grown in confidence and assurance, week by week, as I stood and preached, and knew that it was what I wanted to do full-time.

Being in Heidebeek was like going through withdrawal. Floyd was delighted to hear of our experiences in Britain, but he clearly didn't think they were appropriate to Amsterdam or the work there. Occasionally, we talked at length about it, and I asked him if he would let me go and try. He listened, we discussed it, then he told me that no, the time wasn't right. It was frustrating for me, but I respected Floyd's wisdom and experience, and accepted his decision. I continued to ask God to one day make it possible for me to preach in the streets of Amsterdam, and awaited another opportunity to talk to Floyd about it.

I began making occasional visits to Amsterdam with Paul Filler, a DTS staff member with whom I had become very close, and who shared my enthusiasm for the idea of preaching on the streets. We toured the city together, talking about how we could start a program of open-air evangelism, and praying for God's leading in the matter.

On one visit, as we strolled around, I had a strange experience. The faces of all the people we passed—old and young, cheery and angry, foreign and local—seemed to freeze in the back of my mind. It was like a private slide show, depicting the lostness of the people packed into the city of Amsterdam. God seemed to be saying to me: "Look, John, these crowds are made up of people—people who need to hear about My Son."

I shared my experience with Floyd, and finally he agreed. I could take a small team from the training school onto the streets. My dream had come true!

We began with a series of one-day excursions, piling into a van and driving into Amsterdam from Heidebeek. Once there, we went to one of the squares and sang praise songs before I got up and preached. It was the pattern I had learned in Nottingham, and it was proving effective. We were pleased, as was Floyd, who had joined us out of curiosity. Indeed, he suggested that we extend the scope of what we were doing to include a summer outreach.

I jumped at the opportunity, and began making plans. It would be a four-week event, using a small group of people based out of one of the campsites on the edge of the city. There, among all the drug addicts and travelers, we would establish our base. From there, we would move into the city and do open-air evangelism, inviting those who were interested in learning more to go back to our camp—rather like The Ark under canvas.

Finally, the time for the outreach arrived. After a morning of prayer and praise with the rest of the Heidebeek staff and workers—who had mixed ideas about this type of outreach—my small team crammed into two vans and headed for Amsterdam.

One of our group was Terry Gray, who had discovered midway through DTS that the French center
she had been intending to join was not now beginning as soon as planned. She was now planning to
join the Youth With A Mission center in Lausanne,
Switzerland, where French speakers were needed. In
the meantime, she had a month to kill—and the
Amsterdam outreach seemed like a good idea.

The first days of the outreach went well. We followed the same pattern as before: singing some
lively praise songs as a group, preaching for a few
moments, and then splitting up to try to engage the
listeners in further conversation. There had been
much interest, and already, a fairly constant stream
of young people drifted back to our campsite to hear
more about the Gospel over dinner or coffee.

Ever since Floyd had given the go-ahead for the
outreach, a couple of other staff members from
Heidebeek and I had been traveling regularly into
Amsterdam. We walked up and down the central
city streets, past sex clubs, brothels, cafes selling
drugs over the counter, and teenagers lying stoned
on the pavements.

As we walked, we prayed over every spot where
we planned to preach, claiming each one for God's
power and purposes, and in Jesus' name, shackling
the forces of evil at work there. Because of that preparation, we began to see fruit come from our outreach. People were coming to know Jesus. We were
all excited about what God was doing through us.

"No sex! No violence! No war!" the words were
repeated over and over, like a litany, cutting through
the babble of street chatter and music. A few heads
turned to see where the chanting was coming from,

but most didn't care, or were oblivious to it. It was not uncommon for people to do their own thing on the bustling city streets, or maybe it was just another drug addict overloaded on acid or speed.

But the cry continued, and I sensed that it was more than just another stoned addict. I sought out the source of the sound, and found a man dressed in baggy, flowing clothes. His eyes were glazed with that faraway look that speaks not of drug addiction, but of someone whose life is held in the grip of evil spirits. I talked to him calmly, and he began telling me how his message had come from his guru. When he asked me if I would like to meet his guru, I nodded my head and followed him.

Terry decided that she would go with me, so the two of us eagerly followed along. It was only as we reached the top of the stairs in the old, derelict building a few streets away from the center of town that I realized I had misjudged the situation. Neither of us should have been there, but it was too late; all we could do was pray quietly for God to protect us.

We stepped into a dusty, dark attic room, and immediately we could feel it: a tangible oppressiveness, evil that hung in the air like early morning mist. Four men lounged on cushions scattered across the floor.

In the middle of the room sat the guru: bare-chested, hard-faced, bearded, and suspicious. He took an instant dislike to Terry, and began speaking to her harshly and fiercely. It was like a wave of hatred washed across the room and crashed down on her. I didn't want the encounter to get any more out of hand than it seemed to be, so I stepped in and, with a smile, told the guru what we were doing in the city; how much God loved him, and that he, too, could find a new life in Jesus. A spiritual battle was taking place.

There weren't any takers when we invited them for coffee and more talk out at the campsite. So, after making some excuses, we went back down the stairs and out onto the street. It felt wonderful to be outside in the clear air again; the weight lifted from us, and Terry burst into tears, burying her head in my shoulder.

I was annoyed that I hadn't been more discerning before walking into the confrontation, especially because Terry was involved. She was shaken to her roots. The reality of spiritual warfare was new to her. As I tried to comfort her, I was aware of two things—how I wanted to make her feel safe for the rest of her life, and how I wanted to keep fighting spiritual battles like the one we had just encountered.

The four weeks of the outreach went by almost too quickly, and we returned to Heidebeek, exhausted but happy. We had made an impact on the streets, learning to adapt what we did and how we did it to the climate of the city and the nature of the laid-back, "liberated" people who passed through it.

A good number of people had come to Christ through the outreach. At one stage, we had been asked to move from the campsite, because we were bad for business—the line-up of drug peddlers who used the place as a base for their operations had stopped dealing!

I also returned to the farm with my mind racing over future possibilities; about how we could do things bigger and better the next time. And about what was going to happen with Terry. Our month together in Amsterdam had only deepened my feelings for her, and I couldn't bear the thought of seeing her go off to Switzerland. Yet, while I didn't think twice about shouting out in public how I had become a Christian, I was terrified at the thought of trying to tell Terry privately what I was thinking.

Finally, the time came for Terry to leave. Before she left, she came to talk to me about the incident with the demonic man. I explained to her some more about spiritual warfare, prayer, and the supernatural. We talked for a long, enjoyable time.

As our conversation drew to a close, there was an awkward silence. Then Terry asked: "There's something else we need to discuss, isn't there?"

My insides flipped. She knew! I took a deep breath, and felt my cheeks turn bright red. Hesitantly, I began to tell her how I felt. It wasn't easy, but I stumbled and mumbled my way along. By the time Terry had to board the bus to leave, we had agreed to pray about God's leading in our lives.

I was on cloud nine. Not only was my thirst for evangelism being met (Floyd approved of what he had seen and heard of the outreach, and was now eager to extend open-air evangelism in Amsterdam), but I had been able to tell the girl of my dreams that I was in love with her. Or something along those lines. I had been so nervous that I wasn't quite sure what I'd said!

I began writing to Terry two or three times a week. This was the same John Goodfellow who had rarely managed to write more than a postcard; Mr. Uncommunicative, who discovered that all I wanted to do was sit down with pen and paper and tell Terry all about my days: what was happening at Heidebeek, the things God was showing me, and also encouraging her in her own walk with the Lord.

But the path of true love does not run smoothly, and several months down the road, we hit a pothole. Our still-cautious exchanges sometimes failed to communicate clearly enough, and once Terry ended up spending a day at The Ark on her way through Amsterdam, waiting for me to show up. My absence was seen by her as a sign of my disinterest. I, on the other hand, was back at Heidebeek, not realizing that her visit was either expected or possible. Terry's letters began to taper off, and mine did in return. My heart sank at the thought of her not being interested in me anymore.

I somehow managed to bury my disappointment in the business of life at Heidebeek. There were long prayer walks and busy planning sessions for further evangelism in Amsterdam. Then, seven months later, I found myself on the way to Venice with a team from Heidebeek. Youth With A Mission groups from all over Europe were converging on this water-side city for a program of training and evangelism. Workers from the Lausanne center would also be there, Terry among them.

My hands were cold and sweaty, and my throat was dry as our bus pulled into the campsite just outside Venice. We were greeted by a welcoming "orchestra" of other Youth With A Mission workers, thumping out an arrival symphony on pots, pans, bottles, and cans. There, in the middle of the cheering throng, was Terry. My spirits soared at the sight of her face, then slumped at the thought of what might have been.

I deliberately waited until everyone got off the bus. I was hoping to avoid an awkward encounter with Terry, but she was still there, waiting for me, when I finally stepped out of the bus. One look at her, and I knew that I was still head over heels in love with her.

We greeted each other and managed a stiff hug before I had to go off and arrange accommodations and food for the team. There was much to occupy my mind, but thoughts of Terry began to get in the way.

I eventually got up the courage to invite Terry out for pizza. We started gingerly to explore our feelings again, and my heart soared as I sensed that perhaps there was hope of salvaging my dreams. From that meeting on, we continued to spend time together laughing, talking, and just enjoying each other's company.

Still unsure of myself when relating to women, I sought out the wise counsel of an older Christian man. I told him my problem, and he said, "John, if you believe she's the girl for you, then tell her, and ask her to pray about it."

It seemed a rather direct approach to me, but I believed this man knew what he was talking about, so I followed his advice.

Over a cup of coffee in a noisy cafe, I told Terry: "You know how things have been going between us. Well, Terry, either you are the girl for me, or you aren't. I've prayed about it. Would you do the same?"

I don't know what type of reaction I expected, but it certainly wasn't the one I received! Terry burst into tears. "Well, if it's all or nothing, then I guess it's nothing!" she snapped, as she picked up her handbag and stormed out of the cafe, leaving me with two cups of coffee and a sick feeling in my stomach.

I saw Terry only once after that, to ask her to join the group I was leading on a six-week outreach to Crete. The Venice outreach was coming to an end, and we were preparing to break into smaller teams and head off for evangelism programs all over Europe. Terry refused to join my team, and went instead with a team to Israel.

Fortunately, during my time in Crete, I was kept

busy with leading the team, preaching, and doing follow up, and didn't have much time to dwell on what had gone wrong between Terry and me. During our outreach, we lived on the beaches, and by the time it came to an end, we were all bronzed, fit, and happy at the way God had touched the lives of many of the young vacationers with whom we had come into contact.

At the end of the six weeks, all the teams converged back in Venice. We had a wonderful time sharing stories of our successes, failures, and adventures. It was thrilling to hear the reports, and to see how God had worked through the enthusiasm and open-heartedness of so many students and young people.

My next responsibility, our second summer outreach on the streets of Amsterdam, was already whirring in my mind. I shared the details of it at the gathering in Venice, and appealed for anyone willing to join us to talk to me.

I couldn't resist seeking out Terry, suntanned from her time in Israel, and looking more beautiful than ever. I asked her if she wanted to be a part of the outreach in Amsterdam. She was very noncommittal, and told me she would think it over.

Minutes before our bus was due to leave Venice, Terry came to me. She seemed nervous—something I'd never noticed before.

"I've done a lot of thinking and praying, John," she told me. "And I've realized something...that I really do love you, and I want to come to Amsterdam with you and see what the Lord has for us."

These were the words I'd dreamed of hearing for so long. Now that I was hearing them, they hardly seemed to register. I stared at her, my mouth agape. She smiled as she realized she had caught me so off guard. I finally regained my composure, but by then it was time to board the bus.

Terry waved furiously as I climbed aboard—she would meet me in Amsterdam in just a few days. My heart soared. All I could think of was Terry. I cannot remember a single moment of the trip back to Heidebeek.

16

The Beachhead

It was a great morning, that first morning that we headed down into the red light district. As we neared the quarter of the city that is famous throughout the world for its vice and drugs, we began singing worship songs and clapping our hands. Noise wasn't uncommon in the red light district—there was music and shouting almost around the clock—but our music was of a far different nature. Our singing elicited curious stares from the prostitutes, pushers, and pimps as we wound our way through the narrow streets.

We finally arrived at the edge of the canal beside the Old Church, a beautiful gothic building almost six hundred years old. We stood and looked across the canal to our new home: a narrow, four-storied building squeezed into the most notorious avenue in the whole neighborhood. On one side was a satanist church and a homosexual bar, and on the other, a twenty-four hour porno cinema and drug joint.

We walked across the small stone bridge over the canal and along to the front door of the building. A great cheer went up as I turned the key, unlocked the door, and led the way into the old Budget Hotel.

I was to lead a team of volunteers to renovate the building and then use it as a base for another summer outreach. The prospects thrilled me.

Thirty young people had signed up for the clean-up crew, and among them was Terry. We'd had a year of ups and downs, and were still trying to work out if our future would be spent together or apart.

Another forty volunteers would join us in a few weeks' time for the actual program of evangelism. The people on The Ark opened their doors to us, and gave us room to lay our sleeping bags side by side while work on the building continued.

It was immediately apparent why the Budget Hotel had been so named. Not one penny had been spent on upkeep in years! The building had been used as a cheap hostel for students and travelers, and seemed to have been deserted in an instant when the doors finally closed a couple of years earlier. Plates of half-eaten food littered the table, moldy packages lay in the kitchen cupboards, and empty bottles and grimy hypodermic syringes were scattered all over the place.

Undaunted, we burst into praise and worship. A huge job lay ahead, but just by taking possession of this seedy old place, we had dealt a positive blow for God in this dark area of the city. The battles were not over, but we were establishing a strong beachhead, and sensed God's approval in doing so. After a prayer of thanksgiving, we split into small teams to began the huge clean-up job.

Groups headed off all over the building, which was like a rabbit warren of small, odd-shaped rooms scattered about in no real pattern. In the kitchens, lounges, bathrooms, and bedrooms, we stopped and prayed for God to sweep away any dust of evil that may have settled from the past. We claimed the place and the people who would live, work, and visit in it for God.

I was project manager, and had drawn up a roster of three six-hour work shifts. It was a pattern I'd seen modeled in an Old Testament passage, and one which I felt was appropriate to what we were doing. In addition, those teams not working shared a "prayer patrol" in one of the small rooms at the back of the building. The prayer patrol ran from the moment work started in the morning until the time it ended in the evenings.

We had been impressed while reading the Bible with how Nehemiah had gone about rebuilding the walls of Jerusalem. He had arranged for guards to watch over and protect those who labored on rebuilding the wall. The prayer patrol was our guard. We wanted every hammer blow, every stroke of the paint brush, to spring from and count for God.

It was a filthy job. There were years' worth of dirt and decay to tackle, but no one complained. Quite the opposite—the way the team went about their work characterized all we were hoping to achieve from our new base. We laughed and joked together as we worked, good humor seeming to spill from every room. It was such a marked contrast to the red light district that surrounded us.

Outside our building, there were always plenty of people around, buying and selling drugs or bodies, but there was never a sense of warmth or pleasantness. Because of this, we found our new neighbors were intrigued by our friendliness and evident enjoyment of each other's company. Genuine warmth and laughter seemed so lacking in this part of town.

Also following biblical precedent, we had set a

forty-day limit to complete our work, and just managed to do so. Soon after, the rest of the team joined us for the start of the summer outreach. Their arrival stretched accommodations to the limit, so we devised a system of three tier bunk beds. It meant that people with large noses couldn't sleep on the top bunk, or their nose would brush the ceiling! But with a little care and good humor, we managed to squeeze everyone in.

In the short amount of time we had lived in the red light district, I had begun to sense in a new way the spiritual oppression that hung over the neighborhood like a blanket. It was reflected in the eyes of the people who passed by—eyes that glanced away to avoid contact.

It soon became clear to us that one of the keys to our effectiveness in outreach in this area was the degree to which we responded in the opposite manner to all that went on around us. Instead of furtiveness and secrecy, we needed to display openness and honesty. But that had to begin among ourselves, in the relationships that existed on the team. We were glad to have had the time together, working on the building, to get to know and love each other. We had come through a lot, and were looking forward to what lay ahead.

The renovation job had given the locals time to get used to our presence. There had been some uncertainty on that first day, when we arrived with our songs of praise and worship. We didn't expect the suspicion to disappear overnight. In fact, we were sure there would be much outright opposition in the days to come. But at least they saw we had come to stay. Whatever followed wasn't just going to be a hit-and-run campaign; we were their new neighbors.

At an end-of-renovation meeting, we renewed

our commitment to prayer and spiritual warfare. The importance of these two aspects of Christian service had been impressed upon me early, during my time on The Ark. In fact, after my conversion, I had been told that three of the staff members had spent three days privately fasting and praying for me before I made my commitment.

From that knowledge, my experiences in Nottingham, and the early evangelism forays into Amsterdam, I knew that much of the spiritual battle took place not on the streets, but in the heavenly realm. It was there that bondages and barriers—sexual, emotional, physical, and environmental—were broken down to make an entry point for the Good News about Jesus to come in.

So prayer continued to be an important thrust for our new base, which we named *The Cleft*. The Cleft symbolized the source of fresh water in the desert, like the water Moses found when he struck the rock with his staff. We met together daily for times of worship and intercession, in which we asked God to move against the wickedness so evident around us, and to save those people who were lost.

Sometimes we took these gatherings out into the streets around the area, singing, praising, and praying as we passed the brothels and sex shops. We always seemed to attract curious gazes, furious stares, or outright hostility. There was even an occasional barrage of water or waste from an upper window. People walked the streets in twos, praying for all the premises and people they passed, asking God to prepare their hearts. We believed that when we did go out to proclaim the Gospel, God would bring along those who were ready to respond.

This whole initiative was new territory for Youth With A Mission in Amsterdam. We learned as we

went along the importance of reassessing and revis-
ing the ways we tried to reach out to people so that
they would be more applicable to a person's particular needs. We recognized that we needed to do
more than just sing a few songs on the street and then
expect people to stand and listen to someone talk
about Jesus.

With its famous organ grinders and street per-
formers, Amsterdam has long been known for its
colorful city life. With the garish attractions of the
red light district drawing throngs of tourists, we
needed something more visual than standard group
singing.

As I thought about this, I went back to a biography of William Booth which I had read. I'd been
impressed with his courage and boldness in starting
his mission work in the East End of London. It had
struck me, too, how cleverly the early Salvation
Army had adapted to the times. Today, brass bands
are often dismissed as out of date, but the Salvation
Army originally formed them to play the popular
tunes of the day, to which they had added new words
which preached the Gospel. I talked over what I had
read in the biography with some of the other team
members, and we decided to borrow some of General Booth's ideas. We would hold a "funeral"!

Some of the men on the team disappeared into
the basement of The Cleft and built a giant-sized
coffin. The coffin was then led in a silent, sorrowful
procession through the streets of the red light district, and out into Dam Square, Amsterdam's famous
focal point, right in front of the Royal Palace. By the
time they reached Dam Square, surprising the tourists who had gathered to feed the pigeons, the funeral party had attracted hundreds of interested
men and women. The coffin was set down in the

middle of the square, and as the crowd closed in around it, a man jumped out!

It was Dave Pierce, a young American with a talent for drama and music. Face whitened and wearing dark clothes, he looked just like a corpse. As he sprang from the coffin, he began to shout and scream about how Amsterdam's sex, drugs, and violence had killed him.

All this time, I was on the other side of the square with some of the other team members. We mingled discreetly with the sightseers. As Dave's wails reached a peak, we started singing songs of praise and worship to God, and gradually made our way over to the coffin, cutting a path through the crowd. The people watching didn't have a clue what was going on. Seeing Dave's horrified reaction to our arrival, they didn't think that we were linked in any way.

Finally, as we drew near the coffin, Dave began yelling at me, "Amsterdam ripped me off! There's no hope! There's no meaning in life!"

"But there is hope!" I shouted back, and we began a loud debate about Jesus bringing light into people's dark lives. After a few minutes, we closed abruptly and the "mourners" and "worshipers" turned to talk to onlookers about what they had just witnessed. Those who wanted to talk or hear more were invited back to the small coffee bar we were operating in the main reception area of The Cleft.

The "funeral" became a regular part of our outreach program. Sometimes we acted it out at night, and lit the way with burning torches. The procession never failed to draw hundreds of people. Through this, we saw that it was possible to present striking images that made people want to stop and find out more about what was going on.

We worked on other presentations, too. One was called "The Madman." For this, we held a regular, sober-faced, sing-for-Jesus meeting in the middle of Dam Square. Only a few people stopped to listen, but we didn't expect much else—until I arrived. I waited until the square was fairly busy, and then made my entrance from the other side.

I was dressed in a torn and dirty suit, with my hair disheveled and dusty, and my arms bound at my sides with ropes. Screaming, shouting, and wailing, I ran across to the group, stumbling and falling as I went. I shouted that Jesus couldn't help me, and attacked the "nice little Christian gathering." Naturally, passersby stopped to watch the confrontation—and we won another audience. Many wouldn't leave the square until they prayed for salvation with members of the team.

Another small drama we used involved a human wall blocking off part of the square, with one of us trying to force our way through. It was a poignant symbol of how we can't get into heaven by our own efforts, and it, too, proved effective in grabbing people's attention.

But it wasn't all easy. We came to accept that we couldn't preach the Gospel without risking people's wrath, or offending the unseen spiritual enemy.

On one occasion, I was standing on top of a small table, preaching. A good-sized crowd listened, and I scanned their faces as I talked, watching the familiar reactions: amusement, scorn, intrigue, awkwardness, interest, suspicion, mockery. It never ceased to amaze me how people could stop and watch someone swallow razor blades without thinking a thing about it, but would suddenly become very edgy if someone started talking about God.

Open-air preaching is a little like performing on

a stage. You have to work with your audience well. As I spoke, my eyes constantly darted over the faces of those listening.

One day, as I began telling them about how my life was turned upside down by a seemingly chance encounter just a few hundred yards away, I noticed some kind of disturbance out of the corner of my eye.

Turning, but not breaking my delivery, I spotted three young men stepping through the crowd into the "no man's land" of open space that is always left between a street preacher and his audience. People don't seem to want to stand too close when you're preaching, lest you reach out and try to snatch them into God's hands. When these three young men broke that invisible barrier, I knew it meant trouble.

Help me handle this one, Lord, I asked silently, showing no apparent concern. I had learned that complete outward assurance and confidence is one of the keys to open-air preaching. If you show any indication of not being in control, you lose the attention of your audience.

The three young men marched right up to the table, and tried to drag me down. "Shut up, or we'll make you!" one of them snarled. Later, others told me that the three were heaving and pulling for all they were worth to get me down, but I only felt a light touch.

I continued to speak, ignoring them. *What shall I do now, God?* I asked silently, as I noticed the concern on the faces of some in the audience.

Responding to that quiet-but-clear voice inside, which I've learned to trust, I squatted down until I was face to face with the leader. He was thick-necked, crop-haired, and clearly looking for a fight.

I leaned forward and said to him, as quietly and calmly as I could, "In the name of Jesus, I rebuke and bind you violent spirits, and I command you to leave this square. Now!" I straightened up and carried on preaching, my heart racing, but unafraid.

The light in the eyes of the two accomplices switched off immediately. It was a transformation I had seen often in moments of spiritual confrontation. The leader hesitated for a moment before turning to the crowd with a sneer.

"You know what this guy just said to me? He told me to go away—in Jesus' name!" he uttered in a roar of harsh laughter. "I'm going to go away, but *not* because he told me to!" He shrugged his shoulders and led his two friends away.

Thanking God for His help, I finished the story of my conversion, reflecting again on the commitment I had made. My job was to preach the Gospel on the streets, and I couldn't afford to let anyone or anything intimidate me.

We soon learned that the fear of man was a major stumbling block to effectiveness in street evangelism. If a person on the team was worried or anxious about what people might say or do in response to their sharing the Gospel, their efforts would be shackled. Usually, after a couple of days of experience and plenty of prayer, most people found themselves able to let go of their concerns, and trust God for their safety and their sense of value.

There were rare moments of threatened physical violence, but these were usually resolved by silent spiritual warfare and claiming Jesus' authority over the disruptive spirits.

More common, though, was the emotional aggression we faced from people who were offended by the idea that a God of love should have to die for them because of their failure to live according to His standards. Usually, this could be channeled into positive times of talking and discussion, particularly when we broke up to mingle with the crowds. On some occasions, however, we would be left with an earful of abuse.

There were many days when there was no apparent interest or results from our efforts. At times like that, it was easy to feel discouraged and to question the value of the time and effort being put in, but as we prayed together and asked God for understanding, we were renewed in our determination to keep going and trust God to do the rest.

Yet there were many spiritual victories, and one of them involved the cults that flourished in the city. Amsterdam's whirlpool of drugs and liberal philosophies attracted every kind of fringe religion, all wanting their opportunity to "recruit."

From the time we started doing street evangelism in Amsterdam, I felt that Dam Square was crucial. It was the largest open public space in the city, and hosted fairs, performing troupes, and crowds of sightseers. I felt that Dam Square symbolized "ownership" of the city, and that God wanted it.

So we staged regular prayer walks, agreeing together for the Lord's name to be honored over all others in Dam Square. Soon after, we began to notice that the Hare Krishna and other cult devotees were beginning to stay away. They walked up to the edge of Dam Square from one of the adjoining streets, stopped, and then skirted around the edge of it, as though prevented from coming any closer by an invisible force field.

Even with the excitement of the new ministry in Amsterdam, my thoughts were never far from Terry. Despite the hectic pace, we managed to find the time to be together during the hectic days of renovation and preparation, and I finally felt the confidence to ask her to marry me.

So, one night at The Ark, I took Terry into what had once been the captain's quarters. I had lit a row of candles to create the right atmosphere for what I hoped was the perfect moment. Terry looked more beautiful than ever in the soft glow of the candle-light. I held her hand and told her: "Terry, I love you. I want you to be my wife. Will you marry me?"

"I need some time to think," she responded.

I was taken aback. "But...why...what?"

"I just need time. I have to ask my father," she explained.

"But that could take ages!" I was frustrated at her idea. It would take a long time to go to the States and talk it over with her parents. Terry sensed the direction my thoughts were going.

"No, John. I mean my heavenly Father!" She smiled.

I was still anxious to know, but I reckoned that wouldn't take quite as long. So I smiled and agreed.

A couple of nights later, as we were crossing the River Ij on a ferry, Terry told me: "John, I'm ready to answer you now. Ask me again." The stars twinkled above us, Terry's hair streamed in the breeze, and I asked her again. She answered simply, "Yes." We strolled back to The Cleft that night, hand in hand, with a wedding to plan.

17

Firm Foundations

I swept Terry into my arms and carried her across the seedy threshold into our new home, tiny though it was. Home was a small room tucked away in the rear of The Cleft. It wasn't the quiet, clean place you would normally expect to find newlyweds, but we didn't mind. We were happy, we were together—and we knew God was with us in our marriage.

Ten days earlier, we had exchanged vows and rings in the gardens of Heidebeek. It was a beautiful, crisp, clear fall day, and the fallen leaves had created a carpet of woven gold and amber. It was like the setting of a fairy tale. Then the Bridal March was struck up, and I knew it was more than just a fairy tale—it was a dream come true.

I turned and watched as Terry, dressed in a gorgeous, flowing white dress, was escorted by her father across the leaf-covered lawn toward me. My nervousness at having to remember my lines evaporated at first sight of her.

I stole a glance at my best man, Peter Gruschka, and thought again of all that had happened in the last few years. As Terry smiled at me, I thanked God silently for the wonderful new life He had given me, and for the longing in my heart to tell others about Him.

It felt so good to share this moment with all those who mattered to me. Mom was in the front row, adorned in her best new dress, and beaming from ear to ear like the Queen Mother. Joan and Sean were there, as were Trish and Jamie—a love story from the earlier days of the Nottingham fellowship—and their baby son. Paul Miller and Paul Filler were two of the groomsmen, and standing in front of us to conduct the service was Floyd, looking down with a twinkle in his eye and a smile that threatened to split his cheeks.

Some friends of Terry's performed a dance to a song of worship before we were finally pronounced man and wife. We walked back down the leaf-strewn aisle hand in hand.

During the reception, friends from home, The Ark, and students from the current Discipleship Training School kept coming up to me and slipping things into my jacket pocket. Later, I found wads of money—gifts for our honeymoon—in my jacket pocket.

A wealthy Christian businessman, a friend of Floyd's, made his countryside retreat available to us for the honeymoon. It was a secluded holiday cottage in the hills near the Baltic Sea, not far from the Danish border, and it was all ours!

We were thrilled by this surprise provision, and after our wedding night in a small hotel tucked away in the woods, we set off in a borrowed Audi for our honeymoon destination. On the way, we had an early lesson on our need to trust God together in everything.

It was late in the day, and we were cruising along

the autobahn just outside Bremen. Suddenly, our car began to sputter and slow down. "Quick, pull over!" I told Terry, who was taking a turn at driving. There was an exit just ahead, and she managed to coax the car down the exit and across the intersection, before it finally sputtered to a halt by a small side road.

By now, it was pitch black outside, and we were in a remote spot. There was little traffic, and no sign of help. I looked under the hood and tried everything I knew about car repairs, but to no avail. I climbed back in the car and said, "Come on, Terry, let's pray. God has gotten us this far. He won't let us down now, I know." We bowed our heads together and asked God for help.

We had barely opened our eyes when a small car appeared out of nowhere and pulled to the side of the road in front of us. Terry and I looked at each other in surprise. The driver, a little man with a round, kindly face and sparkling eyes, climbed out and walked back toward us. I started to join him, but he just smiled and motioned me to stay in the car. He went back to his car, pulled a tow rope from the trunk, and connected it to the front of our car. Another smile, and he was back behind the wheel of his car. Before we knew it, we were being towed down the road.

With one eye still on the road ahead, I tried to catch another glimpse of the couple in the car ahead. The woman in the passenger seat turned to look back at us. Her face was wreathed in a kind, encouraging smile. She nodded her head gently, as if to say, "It's okay," as our journey continued. A few minutes later, we found ourselves rolling into a garage with a connecting hotel. We coasted to a halt in the courtyard, and an attendant came over to my window.

I had been distracted with the attendant for a few

moments when Terry called, "John, they've gone!" Sure enough, the couple with the gentle faces had packed the tow rope back into their trunk and were driving off, with one final smile and a wave. They hadn't spoken a single word to us throughout the entire rescue, nor had they waited for us to be able to express our gratitude.

As they pulled away, we turned to each other and said simultaneously: "Do you think that they...." We laughed aloud at having hit on the same idea at once and added the "were angels?" in our heads.

There was no mechanic on duty at the garage, so we were forced to spend the night at the hotel. The next morning, after half an hour of head-scratching under the hood, the mechanic declared that there was nothing wrong, and with a flick of the key, the engine burst to life. We drove on with the consolation of having spent a wonderful stopover in a lovely hotel.

This sense of God's intimate concern and care for us was to prove a rock in the months that lay ahead, for things didn't work out as we had anticipated. Our plan had been to return to Terry's South Carolina home. We wanted to spend time with Terry's parents, friends, and home church so they could get to know me. We also felt that it was vital that our new relationship have some room in which to grow and blossom, away from the busyness of our work in inner-city Amsterdam. I had enrolled in a respected Bible college, as I felt it was important for me to do some more serious studying before moving on further in Christian service.

But our planned week-long temporary stay at The Cleft—between the end of our honeymoon and our flight to the United States—turned into six months. It also heralded the start of another new initiative in evangelism.

My criminal record was the problem. Those past convictions created all sorts of concerns for the authorities whose job it was to give me the paperwork that would allow me to reside in the United States. Extra forms and declarations needed to be completed, and it would take several weeks, if not months, before it was all sorted out. It was a frustration we hadn't expected, but we decided to redeem the lost time by earning some money for the trip.

The Youth With A Mission (YWAM) community agreed to let us stay on at The Cleft, while I once again went onto the building sites to use my bricklaying skills. I found work on a huge civic apartment complex being constructed on the outskirts of the city. However, the work schedule meant I had to be up at 5:30 a.m. in order to be on the site by 7:00 a.m., and I found myself going to bed during the mid-evening to ensure that I got enough sleep—just when Terry, the "night owl," was coming to life. This, accentuated by our cramped quarters, created tension as we learned to love our way around the practical difficulties involved in blending our lives together.

As the weeks stretched into months, the waiting got harder and harder for Terry. All my energies were absorbed in working on the building site, so I didn't have much reserve left for worrying about The Cleft and its ministry. Actually, it was refreshing not to be involved in all the responsibilities of leading such a ministry. My hope was that if and when I returned to such a role, it would be with a freshness and a renewed vigor.

But for Terry, it was different. She wasn't working, and being in and around the building all day, she was more keenly aware of the struggles that were going on as the base we had pioneered several months earlier strove to establish a permanent role. Some of those who had helped in the renovation and summer evangelism outreach were now full-time staff members, but the future direction of The Cleft was somewhat unclear.

The seeds of something new were sown as Terry talked with me in the evenings. She told me how she and other women living at The Cleft were concerned about the prostitutes who worked in the area around our building. The working prostitutes rented windowed rooms in the houses up and down the canal streets where—backlit in a red glow—they sat semi-naked, advertising their "wares" to the passing crowd. When someone wanted their services, they stepped inside and closed the curtains.

Several thousand prostitutes worked this way in Amsterdam's red light district, and the brazenness brought guided tours of vacationers filing through the city's infamous liberal sex shops and brothels.

"These people are our neighbors, you know, John," Terry said one night. "I just don't feel I can walk past them like I do every day—without trying to reach out to them—not without losing my integrity as a Christian. I've got to try. But how?"

I was excited to see her being moved in this way, and we prayed together, asking God to show us the next step.

A few nights later, Terry told me that she and another woman at The Cleft with whom she had been regularly praying, Mientje Brouwer, had set a date on which to go out and try to make contact with one of the prostitutes in the neighborhood. That date was the following Tuesday.

It had been another long and tiring day for me, but that Tuesday night, I almost ran up the steep stairs at The Cleft. I had thought of Terry and Mientje often throughout the day, and wanted to hear how things had gone. Elated, Terry was waiting for me. I made each of us a hot drink, and sat down to hear her story. Her excitement bubbled over as she recounted their first efforts at reaching out to the prostitutes.

Terry and Mientje had begun in prayer. They asked God to lead them to just the right person. They weren't sure what they should do, so they asked the Lord to show them. As they prayed, they felt God impress them to buy some flowers—a Dutch custom when visiting friends—and walk right in and greet the prostitute. And that was exactly what they did.

As they walked around the streets nearest to The Cleft, they found that all the windows were empty. Even though it wasn't a particularly busy time of day, they couldn't find a single girl. They began to wonder if they had heard God wrong. They decided that they hadn't, and that they should keep on looking. Finally, they found a window with a girl in it, and decided that she must be the one to whom the Lord was leading them.

They walked in nervously, and quickly shut the door behind them. They introduced themselves, and told her that they had recently moved into the area and had come to introduce themselves and chat for a while. They handed her the flowers and began a conversation, during which they told her that they were Christians, and about what they were doing at The Cleft.

The prostitute listened intently, not at all anxious to get rid of them. Indeed, she let Terry and Mientje pray for her right before they left, and with tear-filled eyes, told them that she didn't really want to be doing what she was doing, but she needed the money, and couldn't think of any other way to get it.

Terry was elated as she told me the story, but then her eyes dimmed and filled with tears as she recalled the prostitute's dilemma.

"Do you think God can really do something in the lives of people like this, John?" she asked me.

"Sure," I answered her. "It's not easy, of course, but the Holy Spirit can touch the hardest of hearts. He did mine, remember?"

We sat together in our tiny bedroom and prayed for the girls in the scores of windows within close proximity to The Cleft. We asked God to help Terry and the others in their efforts at bridge-building.

Most days after that, Terry and Mientje, followed by other women at The Cleft, either went on a prayer walk, praying for the girls they passed in the windows, or made contact with them. They always took with them a gift of flowers, a thermos of coffee, and some cookies. Sometimes, they met sharp words and stony faces. Other times, they found open ears and broken hearts.

We discovered in a new way the reality of the unseen battle being fought over the red light district. Some evenings when I reached our door, I could sense that Terry had been visiting the prostitutes. There was a presence of evil and wickedness in the room, as though Terry had stepped in something unpleasant and tracked it into the house.

We learned to pray hard and bind the enemy from our home and our lives. Terry began to pray for protection before every visit, and for a special cleansing of the Holy Spirit as she left, so that she wouldn't be adversely affected by coming in contact with people so clearly bound by the enemy.

On some occasions, though, it was a struggle. One particular woman was unyielding and inhospitable—yet Terry felt it was right to keep going back from time to time, trying to show love and care to the woman. "Every time I go in, it's like walking into a mental fog," she told me. "Sometimes I really have to struggle to get the next word out of my mouth. There is a terrible feeling of tightness around my head, just like someone is screwing on a metal band. I find it hard to get my breath, as though there's a great weight bearing down on me. It's scary."

The more that Terry and the other girls from The Cleft spent time with the prostitutes, the better they understood their plight. It made them desperately sad as they saw how often poverty, greed, anger, and rejection were woven into the lives of these women.

There were both young girls with childish faces and teenaged bodies, and older women, some of whom were even grandmothers. Some were illegal immigrants and couldn't get a regular job. Others had been abused or unwanted at home, had run away, and somehow needed to support themselves. Some were supporting their own, or their partner's, drug or alcohol habit. Still others were single parents who needed money to help pay for their children's clothing and meals. One otherwise respectable young wife worked as a prostitute because she and her husband wanted to open a tennis training center and needed the capital!

Six months had elapsed by the time I was finally given clearance to leave for the United States. But Terry and I were no longer frustrated. As we looked back, we could see the benefits of our delay. Terry had been instrumental in beginning a completely new evangelism initiative for YWAM in Amsterdam, and, by the time we left, there were plans to strengthen it with extra workers and prayer support.

We were pleased and excited, and felt that in a way, the work had already been approved by God. The young woman Terry and Mientje had visited on that first morning had not been seen in the red light district since.

Suburban America was a far cry from the maze of prostitutes, brothels, porno cinemas, and sex shops along Amsterdam's crowded back streets. But we quickly adjusted to the airiness, lightness, and freedom, both physical and spiritual, that there was to enjoy in this new setting.

Terry and I rented a second-floor apartment not far from her parents' spacious home. It had wall-to-wall carpets and every utility imaginable, and we reveled in the space it afforded us after the squeeze of The Cleft. The apartment complex had a swimming pool right outside our door, and Terry swam most mornings before having breakfast and going off to work.

It was a time of refreshment and enjoyment for both of us. It was good, too, getting to know Terry's parents. I'd been nervous about what they might think of me, and overwhelmed by the size of their large home and high standard of living. It was such a far cry from the slums of my childhood.

As time went on, Terry's parents and I came to know and love each other. The more I learned about them, the more deeply I respected the love and care they demonstrated for their family, and the faithful way in which they supported their friends and local church. If they couldn't quite understand the way we wanted to live, serving God in a foreign country with little income and no apparent concern for the practicalities of life, then they certainly didn't discourage us.

Almost before we knew it, January had rolled around, and it was time for us to return to Amsterdam. We had kept in touch with Floyd, and had heard from him that YWAM had acquired another large building in the city. It was a former hotel and one-time Salvation Army headquarters, which for years had been overrun by squatters, but had finally been vacated.

The Samaritan's Inn, as it was to be called, stood in the center of the city, adjacent to the Central Station, and on the edge of the red light district, a few snaking streets away from The Cleft. It was a strategic location, and Youth With A Mission had felt led by God to purchase and use it.

The YWAM leaders had asked Terry and me to lead a DTS and head up some new evangelism efforts. So, rested and happy, we flew back to Europe, eager for the new challenges ahead.

One small problem was that we didn't have much financial backing. All Youth With A Mission workers are "faith" workers. There are no salaries. Instead, individual workers seek financial backing from friends, family, and home churches to help meet their living needs. Because of the way our paths had led, Terry and I did not have a great many backers, so we found ourselves with only a few dollars a week to live on.

This clearly wasn't enough to cover the rent on an apartment, particularly in water-ringed Amsterdam, where building development is restricted and apartments are at a premium. But Floyd came to our rescue. "We're still renovating the Samaritan's Inn, but we have a spare room there, if you're interested," he offered.

He took us to see the room. At first, I thought he had shown us the broom closet by mistake! It was small, with no wash basin, and the bathroom was the next floor up. With all the renovation going on, the room was right in the middle of a building site.

After some initial tears from Terry, and frustrated attempts by me to find alternate accommodations, we agreed to move into the room. I constructed a bed on stilts, which meant that we had to climb up close to the ceiling to sleep, but that left space below for living during the day. We could squeeze in two chairs when we had guests, and with some nice pictures on the walls, and Terry's touch, we made it into our home for the next two years.

We asked God to help us be happy with our lot, and He answered our prayers. We came to love our little room, and if we ever complained in our hearts about it, we only had to look at what was happening outside—in the streets around us—to know that it was no accident that we were in Amsterdam.

For God was at work, and we were privileged to be a part of the action.

18

Still Burning

We were running a full program of outreach on the streets of Amsterdam. Music, drama, and dance were all being used to draw a crowd with whom we could share the Gospel. It was tiring, exciting, frustrating, and rewarding...but it still wasn't enough. I felt we needed yet another way of grabbing people's attention, one that managed to capture their curiosity while at the same time making an unequivocal statement as to what we were about.

So we built a huge wooden cross that weighed forty pounds and stood eleven feet tall. Just standing in front of it as we heaved it upright made me realize in a new way what Jesus had done when He died for our sins at Calvary. It made my heart race in thankfulness and gratitude; and I sensed that it would provoke similarly strong feelings out on the streets.

Some were clearly offended by this visual statement. They stopped briefly to shout and curse at us before stamping off. Others stayed to hear what we had to say as we preached from beneath the cross. But the full impact of the cross was only brought home to us when we were visited by someone who knew its power from years of personal experience.

Arthur Blessitt had started walking around the world with his cross twenty years before, and many thousands of miles later, he was still going. By the time he arrived in Amsterdam, he had experienced extraordinary things in scores of countries—and had repeatedly seen the incredible way in which God used the very symbol of His love to touch people's lives and to transform them. Arthur seemed to attract huge crowds from which hundreds knelt right on the streets to commit their lives to Christ. They wept before friends and family, without a thought as to how others viewed them.

Arthur joined our street team for a couple of weeks, and through his involvement, we felt that we should push ahead with our own "cross" plans. We built five more crosses, and teams began carrying them all over the city to meetings and outreaches.

In fact, the crosses became such a common sight in Amsterdam that a visiting German girl stopped and observed to one of our team members that Amsterdam must be a very Christian city, because everywhere she went, she saw people carrying crosses. Alas, she would find as she ventured further around the city that it was quite the opposite. Amsterdam was a city of sin.

One morning, we set up the cross in the open courtyard in front of the Central Station, and I stood in front of it and preached. As I spoke, an angry-looking man stepped from the crowd and pulled the microphone out of my hand. I let him take it, and he threw it to the ground, cursing and abusing me. I stepped back a pace or two to avoid him, raised my voice, and continued speaking. Past experience told me to keep an eye on the intruder, so I kept him in the corner of my focus.

Suddenly he lunged forward, fists bunched to strike my face. I braced myself for the blow—but it never came. Just as his punch was about to connect, he pitched through the air and crashed to the ground, not moving. The meeting came to an abrupt halt as we called an ambulance to take the injured man to the hospital. Afterward, I discovered what had happened.

The abusive intruder had been felled by an ox of a man who was standing nearby. That man wasn't a Christian, but had spent some time talking to Arthur Blessitt in a city park a couple of days earlier, and the encounter had so impressed him that he didn't want any of Arthur's friends to have any trouble!

Arthur's brief visit confirmed to me that the streets were my "pulpit," and that was the way it would stay. Privately, I had sometimes thought that my days of leading street outreaches were limited; that in some way, they were an apprenticeship for when I would be preaching at big missions rallies.

But in Arthur Blessitt, I saw a man totally committed to doing what God wanted him to, who ignored the pressures to do anything else. He was a man walking close to Jesus, who knew that success could not be measured in worldly terms. As a result, the Holy Spirit was able to work miracles through his unassuming, everyday life. I realized that the open air, pavements, and the market squares were what I knew, and where I was most comfortable.

By now, our work in Amsterdam was beginning to attract interest and attention from other YWAM groups, local churches, Bible colleges, and missions organizations around the world. During the summer, we conducted large short-term evangelism projects that drew young people from all over the world.

Many of these young people went back to their home churches, enthusiastic about God and all they had experienced. We also began to get inquiries about taking what we were doing in Amsterdam to new places. Thus a new initiative in evangelism was born: GO Teams, short for Global Outreach Teams.

The idea was to bring together a team of men and women interested in short-term mission work, give them basic discipleship training, ground them in all we had learned about street evangelism, and cement it in place with several weeks of on-the-job training. GO Teams involved us in up to four months traveling each year across Europe, India, and parts of northern Africa, where in cities, towns, even remote villages along the way, we took part in evangelism, working with local churches. Since we were a small, mobile, and independent team, we were able to take the Gospel to even the out-of-way places where the people had as much need to hear about Jesus as those in the towns and cities.

As we planned for these outreaches, it became clear that some of the things we did in Amsterdam were peculiar to that city. We couldn't hope to repeat the funeral procession or the cross march in other parts of Europe with the same results. We needed new ways to draw people. Talented Dave Pierce came up with the solution once more.

He pointed us to *Toymaker and Son*, a musical parable about creation, the fall of man, and salvation through Jesus Christ. It mixes drama and dance into a fifty-minute presentation that has little narration and no dialogue, although its message soon becomes clear. At the end of the presentation, there is a clear opportunity for people to step forward and talk more about what they had just witnessed.

We worked on *Toymaker and Son*, devising a series

of costumes that clearly depicted the different characters, but would also be clearly recognizable in all the places to which we traveled. So it was that I found myself dressed up like an overgrown Pinocchio—complete with knickers and white knee socks—for my part as The Toymaker.

We packed everything into an old 1960's Swedish city bus, and our team of eighteen set off on a four-month cross-Europe trek. We arrived in a village or town about mid-day, and, working through local pastors who had prearranged permits, began preparing for an outreach. Of course, the first thing we always did was to pray with the local Christians.

In the early evening, we began setting up the simple staging and music system in the town square or the largest plot of open land available. This activity quickly drew a crowd, so that by the time we were ready to begin our performance, word of mouth had drawn a large crowd to see these visiting players.

Once the performance and preaching were over, we had conversations that often carried on until well after midnight. Many times, these one-on-one talks were followed with prayer, during which people asked Jesus into their lives. Local Christians translated for us, and invited those who made decisions for Christ to come to church the following week. For several summers, *Toymaker and Son* performed in Spain, Italy, Portugal, Greece, and England.

While in England, we performed in Nottingham. It was strange to be back home, especially wearing my Toymaker costume. But at the end of the performance, I was able to stand up, as I had done so many times before, and point out the places from my past: the wine lodge, the jewelry store that I had robbed, the alleys where I had fought and stolen.

We were packing everything into the bus after one performance, when someone tapped me on the shoulder. "John, it *is* you, isn't it? Johnny Goodfellow?"

I turned around, and there was a friend from the old days. Short and stocky, Terry had been a hard man. As a one-time boxer of some renown, he had not been shy about using his skills outside the ring when the need arose. I was surprised that he had been watching *Toymaker and Son.* We chatted casually for a few minutes, but I sensed we were skirting the real issue. Finally, Terry managed to find the words, "I came down here because I saw you on television the other night. Do you remember?"

I did. A reporter for the local TV station had come down to investigate what we were doing in the town center during our week-long stay. When they learned I was an "old boy" of the town, they had run a short film report about *Toymaker and Son*, including a brief interview with me as the "reformed" villain.

Terry continued, "Well, I was dead surprised to see you like that, and to hear what you were saying. So I decided to come down to see for myself what it was all about. I want to know more, John. You have really changed, you know."

There wasn't time for more talk then, so I invited him to come over to Amsterdam in a few weeks and visit us there. Terry came, and brought his teenage son, James, with him. He told us a story of much pain in his life, including a broken marriage and the temptation of suicide. When Terry and James flew back to Nottingham the next week, they had both given their lives to Jesus.

Another person touched by *Toymaker and Son* during our English visit was a reporter for one of the local newspapers. He contacted me, and we agreed to meet for an interview at a freeway truck stop. For the first twenty minutes or so, his questions were directed at getting information for his article. But for the next ninety minutes, his questions were motivated by his own search. Our coffee went cold as he asked me question after question about God.

But this time, though, the outcome wasn't as encouraging. When we finally parted, the reporter told me: "I believe it's all true, you know—everything that you've said about Jesus dying for our sins and all that. I believe it. It's just that I can't give what it demands of you. I like women, you see, and I'm just not prepared to make that kind of sacrifice. I don't want to become a monk."

In the early days, such a response would have troubled me greatly. But over the years, I had met every kind of response to the Gospel. As well as conviction and tears of joy and laughter, there had been venom, scorn, ridicule, disinterest, unbelief, and suspicion. I had learned not to worry, but to trust God to work in the lives of those we met, and at His own pace. Perhaps this contact would be the first of many that would eventually lead this man to Christ. Or perhaps he had already made his choice. It wasn't for me to try to work it all out. It was for me to keep on going, talking, praying, and trusting for God to prepare the people with whom I came in contact, and I must leave the rest to Him.

Over the past few years, I have preached on the streets hundreds of times. Usually, I share God's love in the only way I really know how; by telling folks about what happened to me when I found myself at the end of my rope, and God stepped in. I have told the same story so many times that I could almost recite it in my sleep.

Yet every time I tell my story, it is fresh to me. I recall those days and nights of lostness, loneliness, and emptiness when I was desperately trying to fill the hollowness with drugs, alcohol, sex, and occult experiences. As I retrace my steps, my heart fills with joy at knowing that God hasn't just changed my life—He has literally saved it.

I am certain that if God hadn't intervened in my life that day near Amsterdam's Central Station, I would be dead by now. My anger, violence, and desperation were spinning out of control, and it would not have been long before they pitched me into something too far, too wild, and too late.

Every time I speak to people, be it a crowd or an individual, these thoughts and feelings spill around inside me. It's a simple love for Jesus and all that He has done for me, and it is thrilling to be part of something that changes someone's life for all eternity. Before I start to preach, I always remind myself that there will be people listening who will respond and commit their lives to Christ, people who had no idea what was going to happen to them when they left home in the morning!

Take, for example, a man in Rome who happened to meet our GO Team. He had taken a stroll with his daughter to get ice cream when he was attracted by the noise and the crowd. *Toymaker and Son* was in town. Drawn to the drama, he paused to watch for a few minutes, and found himself gripped. Later, he told us that he simply couldn't pull himself away.

Following the performance, he and his daughter were among the first to step forward and ask to be prayed for to accept Jesus as their Savior. The very next evening, he returned to the square with his wife and other daughter, and wept tears of joy as they, too, chose to become Christians.

Then there was Danny. He was planning a murder when he and his wife strolled past a street team in Amsterdam's pretty Vondel Park. A well-known criminal in the city, he had been ripped off by an associate, and was scheming a way to make the man pay with his life. But as he heard me preaching about how I had been a thief and a criminal, his ears pricked up. He and his wife both stopped to listen to what I had to say. When approached by one of our team members afterward, first his wife and then Danny bowed their heads and prayed for forgiveness of their sins.

Libby wasn't looking for anything more than a good time when we bumped into her and a friend near Dam Square. The two had paused to stare at an open-air rally being conducted by another group of Christians. Together with a friend, I began chatting with them, and later that night at The Ark, Libby said a simple prayer of commitment. The result was dramatic. When she arrived for work on Monday morning, she was surrounded by her friends, all clamoring to know what had happened to her over the weekend. They told her that she looked incredible. With a glow on her face, Libby was able to tell them how she had met Jesus.

There are many more stories that come to mind, of people physically healed by the Lord, people set free from terrible bondages of evil, people released from deep emotional hurts from their past, and all through coming to know Jesus. But I don't want to end this book by telling you another story. Instead, I want to close by challenging you to take the opportunity of starring in your own story.

If you have read this far and you are not a Christian, you need to decide whether you think what I've recounted is fact or fantasy. If you accept that it is true, then I believe you need to respond by giving your life to Christ. There's a brief prayer to help you do this in the Afterword. You can turn there right now.

If you are already a Christian, then I hope that you have finished this book having been encouraged in one of two areas, or perhaps both.

First, I believe God can use you to reach those in your family who do not know Him. Even if there are big barriers, God can repair relationships so that you are able to share the Gospel through word and action. It may take time and some tears, but I am convinced that after we have been restored to our heavenly Father, He wants to see us restored to our earthly fathers, mothers, sisters, brothers, and children.

Secondly, I want you to be stirred for evangelism: to see that every day, there are countless people who are lost and hurt, who through a "chance" encounter—because someone left a purse behind, or they were out buying ice cream—get to hear the fantastic message of salvation.

All they need is for someone along the way to be available to them. That's the key: availability. Not personality, or ability. Not everyone is called to street evangelism and open-air preaching—although I've found through short-term mission initiatives that once many try it, they wonder why they took so long to become involved!

It is simply a question of responding to Jesus' commission in Matthew 28, when He said: "All authority in heaven and on earth has been given to me. Therefore go and make disciples of all nations."

You may have to go to a foreign city, thousands of miles from home; or to your local shopping mall on a Saturday with a drama team or singing group; or to a mothers-and-toddlers support group, where people are looking for friendship; or to your school or office, where the name of Jesus is known only as a curse word.

But whatever you do, don't leave it for someone else to do.

One summer recently, I felt the Lord calling me to walk with a cross in Africa. I trained for several weeks, lugging a backpack full of bricks around the streets of Amsterdam. Then I packed a few spare clothes and flew to Zambia.

For two weeks, I carried a large cross down into the center of the city each day, praying and preaching. My team was made up of five local people, including a housewife and a teenage girl. About five hundred people gave their lives to Christ while I was there, and it was exhilarating to be around as people responded to the Gospel so openly.

I expect there will be other trips like that in the future. I hope so! New initiatives in evangelism continue to develop in Amsterdam, with teams going into Eastern Europe, the Soviet Union, and other areas with people who have been unreached by the Gospel. The GO Teams continue to operate year by year. Other young evangelists and leaders are emerging, and it is exciting to see the ways in which God is using and leading them.

Terry and I now have two sons, Sandy, eight, and Jason, three. When they grow up, we have an idea tucked away in the back of our minds. We've even begun to put a little money aside for it.

If we eventually retire, we want to buy an RV and do some touring around Europe, America, and maybe even Australia. We could be free agents, stopping and starting and going where we're needed, meeting up with other folks along the way— befriending them and sharing our treasure—Jesus!

After all, I hadn't really heard the Gospel until I was in my mid-twenties. But as it was revealed to me, I fell in love with the simplicity of it all, and how Jesus died for me.

I know there are lots of other people just like that. They may have heard a little about Jesus, but they've never really heard the truth. I figure that there are lots of older folks who need to be told, too—in a manner that's appropriate to them.

If it does work out that way, maybe I will finally get around to making that overland trek to the East I had planned once before. But this time, I will already know where I'm going, and I'll have found what I was looking for.

Afterword

If you have read this far, then I hope you have understood a little about how Jesus can transform your life—even today, even now.

If you have questions, please talk them over with someone—perhaps a Christian friend who may have given you this book to read. Talk with a relative or a work colleague who's a Christian, or go to a church this Sunday and ask to talk to someone afterward.

You can turn to the Bible, too. As God's timeless word, it tells how we have become separated from Him through sin—but it also points to the way back, through Jesus. Take some time to read and study it for yourself, perhaps starting with the gospel of John. Ask God to help you understand it.

Perhaps you think that you're okay because you have never done anything as wicked as the things I did. Well, that is not what the Bible says. It states that every one of us has fallen short of God's mark. "For all have sinned and fall short of the glory of God," says Romans 3:23. That includes every one of us.

Or perhaps your life has taken you to even darker corners of life—and you think you've gone too far for God to forgive you. As surely as the Bible says all have sinned, it says *all* can be forgiven. There is a promise which says: "If we confess our sins, he is faithful and just and will forgive us." That covers you, too.

Do you want to experience that forgiveness in your life? I hope so. Perhaps you want to think it over first—or maybe you are ready to receive it right now. You can.

Just pray this short prayer, right now:

"Father God, I believe that You have been speaking to me and showing me that I am separated from You by sin. I believe that Jesus Christ, Your only Son, was crucified and rose from the dead, taking my punishment so that I may be forgiven. I ask You to forgive all my sins in His name, and I ask Jesus to come into my life and take control. I turn my back on all that has passed, and offer my life to You from this day on. I thank You that You are answering my prayer even now, through the power of Your Holy Spirit. In Jesus' name, Amen."

If you have prayed this short prayer from your heart, congratulations! Welcome to the family!

But don't keep it to yourself. Tell some Christians you know. If you don't know any, find some! They will want to encourage and help you on the journey ahead.

For further information about Youth With A Mission, please write to:

Youth With A Mission, Amsterdam
U.S. Support Office
4931 Lori Ann Lane
Irvine, California 92714

or:

Youth With A Mission
North American Office
P.O. Box 55309
Seattle, Washington 98155